To An Most Awesome Pastor, Woman of God Michelle, You have TRULY IMPACTED my Life!

Love,
Cheryl

# *The Re-Making of An Addict*

Cheryl Thacker-Brown

authorHOUSE®

AuthorHouse™
1663 Liberty Drive
Bloomington, IN 47403
www.authorhouse.com
Phone: 1-800-839-8640

© 2011 Cheryl Thacker-Brown. All rights reserved.

No part of this book may be reproduced, stored in a retrieval system, or transmitted by any means without the written permission of the author.

First published by AuthorHouse 7/1/2011

ISBN: 978-1-4567-5600-0 (e)
ISBN: 978-1-4567-5601-7 (hc)
ISBN: 978-1-4567-5602-4 (sc)

Library of Congress Control Number: 2011907092

Printed in the United States of America

Any people depicted in stock imagery provided by Thinkstock are models, and such images are being used for illustrative purposes only. Certain stock imagery © Thinkstock.

This book is printed on acid-free paper.

Because of the dynamic nature of the Internet, any web addresses or links contained in this book may have changed since publication and may no longer be valid. The views expressed in this work are solely those of the author and do not necessarily reflect the views of the publisher, and the publisher hereby disclaims any responsibility for them.

# ACKNOWLEDGMENTS

I take this time to thank and acknowledge God for Who He is in my life. All that I am is because of Him. In Him, I have more than I could ever hope for. Without Him, I am nothing.

I also thank my praying mother, Mattie. She taught me how to be a woman who fears God. Had she given up on me, I'm sure the grave would have claimed me.

I thank my children, Nadia Nicole, Pierre Hassan, and Desiree Dominique for always loving me no matter what. I thank my other children, JeNae Dashawn, LaMeka Andrea, and David Jr, for accepting me as "Mom-Miss Cheryl". To my grandchildren, Terry, TraNae, Isaivian,(& the one on the way)---you're the best! To my Reesie---never had a friend like you; never will again. To Vanessa(Neen)-you were there "way back when". You're always in my heart. To my son-in-law, Donald-thanks for taking care of my Nadia.

Now to some very special people who thought I was their inspiration, but really, they were mine: Sharon Damiani(you said "Mrs. Cheryl, you should write a book!"), Lorraine, Amber, Christi, Tish, Meesh, the Ervins, Tiffany, Aaron, Iris, Lacey, Tammy, Lisa Hut, Sandy Manlove, my godsons Tray, Eric, Jonathan, and Carlos, my goddaughter Mya "My Ceta", "Miller" (my Homey), Pastor Brian C. Dean & family, Rev. Prince A. Davis, my father Willie, ALL of my siblings, the late Bishop Nathaniel L. Henry, Apostle Linda D. Henry, Heavenly Place COGIC, the Mt. Gilead family, HGM family, Gary & Lillian DeFrance, Dawn & Mike Sheehan, David & Sharon, Ms. Brandy & "Chubby Wubby", Vincent, Laqwin, Brandon, Ky'ree, Daylynn, Shaylynn, Shawn, Sis. Florence, Jacqui, and the late

Doreathea("Tiny")---without all of you, my life would have been less meaningful. **I LOVE YOU ALL!!!**

Finally, to the only man that was able to tie me down; the only man whose kisses I "get lost" in; the only man who can make me laugh without saying a word; the only man who can exasperate me with one gesture; the only man who rode me in a horse and buggy; the only man who ever made me feel like a princess ---my "Day-Day", Deacon David A. Brown, Sr.

There is a KING in you, and you still give me butterflies! Thanks for supplying me with some of the greatest lessons I've ever learned. **I LOVE YOU BEYOND WORDS!**

# Contents

| | |
|---|---|
| INTRODUCTION | ix |
| PART ONE: THE FORMATIVE YEARS | 1 |
| CHAPTER ONE: SOME THINGS YOU NEVER FORGET | 3 |
| CHAPTER TWO: LEARNING TO LIE | 7 |
| CHAPTER THREE: INFLUENCED BY DEVILS | 11 |
| CHAPTER FOUR: TRAPPED IN A SPELL | 15 |
| CHAPTER FIVE: TEENAGE WITCH | 19 |
| PART TWO: THE ADDICTION BEGINS | 23 |
| CHAPTER ONE: SOLD OUT TO SATAN | 25 |
| CHAPTER TWO: TOO FAR GONE | 29 |
| CHAPTER THREE: SATAN'S SECRET AGENT | 33 |
| CHAPTER FOUR: DEVIL IN DISGUISE | 37 |
| CHAPTER FIVE: THE NIGHTMARE BEGINS | 39 |
| PART THREE: AND THEN THERE WAS CRACK | 43 |
| CHAPTER ONE: UNHOLY DESIRES | 45 |
| CHAPTER TWO: INSANITY | 49 |
| CHAPTER THREE: RUNNING INTO A TRAP | 53 |
| CHAPTER FOUR: WHEN CRACK CALLS | 57 |
| CHAPTER FIVE: CAUGHT AND CONTROLLED | 61 |
| PART FOUR: A NEW BIRTH | 67 |
| CHAPTER ONE: HEARING GOD'S VOICE | 69 |
| CHAPTER TWO: CRYING OUT TO GOD | 73 |
| CHAPTER THREE: GETTING RID OF THE OLD | 75 |
| CHAPTER FOUR: YIELD NOT TO TEMPTATION | 79 |
| CHAPTER FIVE: ISSUES | 83 |

| | |
|---|---|
| PART FIVE: FROM THEN UNTIL NOW | 87 |
| CHAPTER ONE: LIVING BY HIS PRECEPTS | 89 |
| CHAPTER TWO: NEW DIRECTIONS | 93 |
| CHAPTER THREE: WHERE HE LEADS ME I WILL FOLLOW | 97 |
| CHAPTER FOUR: NEW HORIZONS | 101 |
| CHAPTER FIVE: A BRAND NEW LIFE | 105 |

# INTRODUCTION

There are things in life that happen to us that we have no control over. Things like which parents we have, where we grew up as a child, who our siblings and other family members are, and how we were raised as children are things we usually have no say about. Yet, these things shape us into the adults we are to become. Good, bad, and/or indifferent, we all are a product of how we were raised.

When a child is damaged at a young age, what becomes of that child? How do you recover from abuses that you received at the hands of the ones who were supposed to nurture you? What happens to the child with an absentee father? What happens to the child that looks for love in all the wrong places, and winds up strung out on drugs, with no where and no one to turn to? What happens to the child who acquires addictive personalities that they believe are "normal"? Can they ever recover?

In this book, you will see how an all-loving God rescues a woman who thought there was no way out of the hole that she had dug for herself.

# PART ONE: THE FORMATIVE YEARS

# CHAPTER ONE:
# SOME THINGS YOU NEVER FORGET

*"The heart is deceitful above all things, and desperately wicked: who can know it?"* Jeremiah 17:9

I was born March 8th, 1967 at Morrisiana Hospital in The Bronx, New York. I was the fifth child of my mother, and the tenth child of my father. I don't remember much about Crotona Park, where I lived for the first two years of my life, but I remember 544 St. Paul's Place. (My being able to remember all the way back to two years old is a miracle in itself, but I'll explain that later.) I can remember the day the moving van brought our furniture to our third floor apartment. They brought in the long sofa first, then a smaller one. The third piece was curved, as it was part of a sectional sofa. The long piece was first, the curved piece next, then the smaller sofa. But, all my little mind could conceive was that the moving men had bent my Mama's sofa! I started hollering and screaming, as though the world would end. I just couldn't understand why Mama wouldn't "make that dumb ole' man take that dumb ole' couch back, and get us a new one!" And I told Mama so, too. I wasn't ashamed to say anything back then. I knew Mama would let me get away with anything – except temper tantrums. I guess I was a little bit crazy from the start because I threw them anyway. My behind still remembers the butt whippings I got from throwing temper tantrums. Some things, you never forget.

My oldest sister, who was sixteen years my senior, had my niece, Ressie, when I was two. Mama worked as our sole provider. She worked a lot. My Dad was never around much, so my big sister took care of me. She gave me baths and washed my hair, taught me my alphabet and how to count, took me to the park and played with me, put me to bed at night, and literally acted as if I were her own child – until Ressie came. Then, I was kicked to the curb. We couldn't play games like chase in the park anymore because we couldn't run off and leave Ressie. I couldn't sing as much around the house anymore because I would wake Ressie. I couldn't sleep with my sister anymore because Ressie took my spot. Ressie, Ressie, Ressie! That's all I ever heard, and I was pretty darn mad about that.

 I came into the world on my parents' seventeenth wedding anniversary. Mama was thirty-eight and Daddy was thirty-nine. Daddy was very dark-skinned in color, but Mama had a light complexion. All my older siblings have my Mama's complexion, but I'm dark like Daddy. Ressie looked almost white, and she was as adorable as a baby doll – and I hated her. She took my place. I was no longer the favorite around the house. Nobody told me how cute I was like they use to before Ressie came. Nobody made a big fuss over me anymore, and at a very early age, I developed a very low self-esteem.

 As we grew older, my brother started calling me Aunt Jemima. She was the lady on the pancake box. The box was bright yellow, and Aunt Jemima was so black she looked like an ink spot. Whenever Ressie and my brother wanted to make me mad, which seemed like all the time, they would call me Aunt Jemima. And oh! How we would fight! I use to hate to look at myself in the mirror. All I saw was what Ressie and my brother told me I was – a black, ugly girl whom nobody could stand. Around four or five years old, I got the notion that Noxema, a skin cleanser, would make my skin lighter. So, every night I'd cake it on my face, hoping to wake up in the morning looking like everybody else in my house. After months of this, I finally said, "What's the use! I'm just black and ugly!"

 In the Word of God, King David says in Psalms 51:5, "**BEHOLD, I WAS SHAPEN IN INIQUITY; AND IN SIN DID MY MOTHER CONCEIVE ME**". The Bible lets us know that because of one man's disobedience, sin entered into the world and it is natural for man to sin (Genesis chapter 3; Romans 5:12; 7:14-23). The events of my life have caused me to understand that the Devil (Revelation 12:9), the adversary of God and His people (1Peter 5:8), starts early in the life of a person who has been ordained by God to do great works for Him. Rejection and low self-esteem are the tools he used on me.

 I can remember thoughts of hatred and feelings of rage racing through my mind and I began to be mean. I would take my anger out on my niece.

No one ever suggested that I be mean to her and nobody ever used the word "hate" in my house. It wasn't allowed. At no time did my sister ever tell me that I was not loved or loved less once Ressie was born. In fact, as I look back, everybody tried to make me feel special once they saw my jealousy of Ressie. But, it was all to no avail because I hated her and everybody knew it.

Where did this fierce hatred come from? Where did this low self-esteem and rejection come from? From the one who, for twenty-seven years, tried to keep me from walking in God's plan for my life: Satan (Job 1:6). He is a liar and the father of lies (John 8:44), and he will say and do anything to try and stop God's purpose in our lives. If he can convince us that we are worthless and that we'll never amount to anything, then sometimes, it's difficult to believe anything else.

It is important to have a close personal relationship with Jesus Christ, and to be filled with the Holy Spirit. He teaches us God's will, guides us into all truth, and will show us our future (John 14:26; 16:13). My mother loved God and she took us to church. She wanted all of her children to live as Christ wants us to live, and we did, but only when she was looking. She worked a lot to keep a roof over our heads and my father was never home. Whenever he was, he seemed very mean. He smoked cigarettes and he drank. Pretty soon, so did my older three siblings.

With Mama being gone so much, our house seemed like the neighborhood hang-out spot. All I saw and heard was drinking, smoking, and cursing. The house always smelled of marijuana, music blared from the record player all day, and it would be filled with people who looked and acted strangely. We would peek through the keyhole of our bedroom door to see what was going on because we weren't allowed around the grown-ups. When people knocked on the door, my sister would say, "DISAPPEAR!" After a while, as soon as we heard a knock on the door, we'd be gone before she could say it.

Having to be "hidden" all the time aroused my curiosity. So, I would lie at times and say I had to use the bathroom just so I could get out of the room. Once, I got to the bathroom door, and it wouldn't open. I knocked on the door, and then I started to bang because this time, I really had to go. But, there was no answer. I yelled for someone to help me and my sisters came running. Some man was in there, but he wouldn't answer when they called his name, and he wouldn't open the door. Another man came from the living room and finally, he pushed open the door, breaking the lock. The toilet was right next to the bathtub. There was the man, sitting on the toilet with his pants around his ankles, slumped over the tub with a needle sticking out of his arm.

That image has never left me.

Some things, you just never forget.

I was six years old.

# CHAPTER TWO: LEARNING TO LIE

*"Behold, thou desirest truth in the inward parts"*
*Psalms 51: 6a*

Those early days on St. Paul's Place taught me how to lie and to lie well. No matter what, we never told on each other. My brother, my niece and I would do all kinds of crazy stuff, things we knew we were not supposed to do, and when we got caught, our famous answer to the question, "Who did this?" was "I don't know!"

"Who broke my shoe?"

"I don't know!" – That was me and Ressie. When my sister would fall asleep after drinking all day, we'd play dress-up.

"Who was in my room?"

"I don't know?" – That would be my brother in our oldest brother's room. He would sneak peeks at my brother's "dirty books", as we called them. Of course, he'd bring them out to show us, too.

"Who keeps knocking on this bathroom door?"

"I don't know?" – That would be all of us. We'd take turns knocking on the door and running.

No one taught us to lie. It was natural. Isn't it annoying that you have to be taught how to read and write – something that will help you to be successful – but sin, which will send you to hell, comes naturally? We were taught to always tell the truth, but all we did all day was lie. Then, we learned how to take things without asking, which was stealing. Oh, sure, even at seven, I knew it was wrong to steal, but I sure got a kick out of it. My sister was mean to us when she'd drink. She would yell at us and curse so badly, and we were terrified of her. To pay her back, I would take her things and move them around – anything to aggravate her as much as she aggravated me. Remember – this was the sister that took such good care of me until Ressie came.

Once my niece was born, I noticed that my sister would sleep a lot. Not get in the bed and sleep – she'd be talking to us and all of a sudden, she'd nod off. My other sister did this often, too, and we would laugh because they looked so stupid! If they heard us, they would pop their heads back up and we'd shut-up real fast so as not to get beat.

We got beat a lot. For every little thing. For not flushing the toilet. For playing in our hair. For talking when we were told to go to sleep. For playing. What kid gets beat for playing? Isn't that what kids are supposed to do?

From a young age, I was absent-minded. I forgot everything and my mind would wander all over the place. But I could always think up the most foolish things to do. The beatings we got were merciless. You would think that those beatings would cause me to walk the straight and narrow path, wouldn't you? Well, not me! I was a daredevil. I knew the risk of getting caught, but I'd try it anyway.

One time, I saw a commercial of this beautiful white woman sitting in a beauty salon on television. She started out with long hair, then, she had a short hairstyle. She looked even prettier with short hair and all her friends on the commercial said so. So, I decided to cut my hair! Maybe then I'd be beautiful to everyone, too. Mama and my sister always kept my hair in three pigtails, two on each side and one on top. I had shoulder length hair, and I cut the pigtail on the left. It was braided and I cut it all the way to the beginning of the braid. I was so proud! I ran into the living room holding my braid in my hand, excitedly saying, "Look, 'yall! Ain't I bootiful? I cut my hair!" – and the room grew absolutely silent. Ressie and my brother whispered a low "Ooooo!", and my sister jumped up and wore my little behind out!

I couldn't understand why I was getting a spanking. All I was trying to do was be pretty like everybody else. I tried to explain in between hits, but I was told to shut-up. When my sister said shut-up, you shut-up. I could never explain myself. None of us could. We were told all the time that children were to be seen and not heard. And I began to grow angrier. The devil had planted a seed of rejection and low self-esteem had taken control.

Most of the time, I would think to myself, "I'm just ugly and stupid, and ain't nobody ever gonna' like me anyway, so I'm just gonna' hate them, too!" I would do stuff just to get even with my sister. I couldn't take my anger out on her, so I took it out on Ressie. I'd stick my foot out as she walked by. I'd break her toys and lie and say I didn't do it. I'd pick fights with her all the time. She was a bit chubbier than me, so we'd fight like cats and dogs. One thing about it – she never let me get the best of her. She stood her ground no matter what.

As I write this, I realize how severely I could have damaged her self-esteem. I've asked her forgiveness many times for the mean way I use to treat her back then. I had no idea what I was doing. Maybe if I had someone who was able to hear from God at home with us more often, a lot of things could have been avoided.

Mama had no idea what went on in our house all those many hours she was gone. My sisters would burn incense to kill the marijuana smell, and they'd open up all the windows to air out the house before Mama came home. We were never crazy enough to tell on any one of them. Once, after getting beat for something that I can't even remember, I threatened to tell Mama when she came home. My sister grabbed me by the arm, lifted me off the floor, and beat the mess out of me. She said I'd better not tell Mama anything about what goes on while she was gone. If I did, she said I'd get a worse beating than the one she gave me for just saying I was going to tell. So, telling Mama was not an option.

My sisters drank all the time, and they smoked marijuana even more. What I didn't know back then was that they also used heroin. That was the reason they would nod all the time. Once, as we were taking a nap, I awoke, having to go to the bathroom. All I heard was music from the front room. Ressie and my brother were still asleep. I knew we weren't alone. We never were. I eased out of our room, tip-toed to the living room, and saw my sister and two other people sprawled out on the sofa, fast asleep. I tipped my way into the bathroom as quiet as I could be. I was scared to flush the toilet because I didn't want to wake anybody. I'd get in trouble for that. I also didn't want to get in trouble for not flushing the toilet. As I was trying to figure out what to do, the door eased open. My heart jumped into my mouth. I knew I was in for it, now! I started crying, just knowing it was my sister with the belt. I often wish it would have been.

A man with white hair and a white beard, who was a regular in our house, appeared around the bathroom door with his finger up to his mouth.

"Sshh, don't be scared, Cherie. I'm not gonna' hurt 'cha", he said. I was relieved. I thought my behind was going to be beaten for sure. He picked me up and hugged me, and I felt safe for a minute. As I said, my Dad wasn't around much, so I didn't get hugs from men. As I saw him all the time, I thought for sure this man would never hurt me. But, I began to get scared again. Even though he was telling me that I was pretty and that made me feel good, his hands started reaching under my skirt. He was breathing heavily in my ear and his breath smelled like alcohol. I was trying to squirm out of his arms, afraid of his hands intruding my lower body, also afraid to yell. He kept saying I'd get beat if I woke my sisters up, and that they wouldn't believe me if I told them what was happening. I knew he was right on both counts, so I held my screams in as his fingers went inside of me. But, something in me said the heck with getting a beating. This was a million times worse than any beating I ever got, and I bit him. Hard. I don't even remember where I bit him. I just bit him, he dropped me to the floor, and I got up and ran back to my room.

    I never said a word to anybody in the house about it.

    I told you – I learned how to lie and lie well.

# CHAPTER THREE: INFLUENCED BY DEVILS

*"For I know the thoughts I think towards you, saith the Lord, thoughts of peace, and not of evil, to give you an expected end"*
*Jeremiah 29:11*

As I look back at those early years, I realize that there is no greater power than God. Satan targeted me for destruction from birth, but God ordained His purpose for me long before the world began (Romans 8:29-30). God knew me before He formed me in my mother's womb (Jeremiah 1:5). He kept angels around me (Psalms 91:11), so that the enemy could not completely destroy me. But oh, how he tried to stop God's plan for my life.

Those early incidents caused me to feel like I was nothing. I felt ugly and dirty all the time and I didn't think anyone could or would help me. I was scared around the house even more now, and I didn't dare tell anybody. I felt like it was all my fault. If I'd had just said that I had to go to the bathroom, then, just maybe "it" wouldn't have happened.

Anyone who says that children are not tormented by demons has not been well informed. The devil talked to me quite often. At the age of seven, not long after the bathroom thing, I began to see and hear strange things. Already feeling unloved and not liked, I would hear voices that said that I was just an ugly, useless, black nothing. Accepting Satan's lies as true, I began to act according to how I felt. I rarely remember myself just smiling.

I laughed when playing with my niece and my brother, but I never smiled. I was always sad and unhappy inside.

At night, I would see shadows fly across the room. I would become so terrified that I couldn't sleep. It seemed as if animals were everywhere, and I was sure there were people walking around in the room. Whenever I'd awaken my niece or my brother, they never saw or heard a thing. I don't think I really knew anything about people being crazy back then, but I believed I was because the voices kept telling me I was.

As time passed, the terror at night got worse, but I stopped trying to tell people about it. Eventually, I learned to overlook the people I saw at night. I had made up in my mind that if they were going to hurt me, they would have done so already. So, I just tuned them out. They were still there, but I pretended as if they weren't. I grew accustomed to them, and after a while, I began to speak back to them. When I got tired of their constant harassment, I'd tell them to shut-up and go away. They'd be angry, but they did what I said. Back then I didn't understand why they obeyed me. I just knew they did, and I began to tell them what to do.

To some of you reading this book, you may be thinking, "This lady's crazy!" But, to others, who may have experienced or are even now experiencing similar things, **YOU ARE NOT CRAZY!** The spiritual world is very real, and if you are one of God's "called out ones", the devil will do anything he can to stop you from walking in your purpose. I had no idea who I was in Christ until I was twenty-seven years old. Because no one in my life could see what was going on in the spirit world, the devil and his demons led me down a path of destruction. All the devil needs is an opening. Once he gets one, he will continue to build on it, in order to hinder God's purpose in our lives.

With Mama working all the time, and my sisters caught up in their own world, I was left to my own devices. I started sneaking around, doing things that no normal eight or nine year old child should be doing. It felt good to lie, and hatred was now a part of my nature. The devil had already started his plot to cause my demise, and it seemed as if nobody cared or even noticed.

In 1Samuel 28, the Bible records the story of King Saul and a witch. It is proof that demons do exist. There is also the account found in Mark 9:14-24, where we see a man bringing his son to Jesus because the boy was tormented by demons. The text says the boy had been possessed since he was a child. It is Satan's desire to deceive us into believing that he does not exist and that things of this nature do not take place today, but he is a liar and there is no truth in him (John 8:44). His primary target is children, and through this book, I intend to expose him.

If you are reading this book, it is not by chance or by coincidence. God needs you to understand that He has given you power over all the power of the enemy and that nothing by any means shall be able to hurt you (Luke 10:19).

God is calling you to be an intercessor for children who have no defense against the devices of Satan. If you have been a victim of his wicked schemes, this book will teach you how to use the Word of God to break every stronghold in your life.

# CHAPTER FOUR: TRAPPED IN A SPELL

*"The snare is laid for him in the ground, and a trap for him in the way"* --- Job 18:10

There are biblical accounts that reveal Satan's plans to assassinate the people of God. In Exodus 1:10-22, an Egyptian king made a decree to kill every male child born to the Israelites. He inwardly feared their power, but he also was inspired by demonic forces. Moses was born at this time. God would later use him to lead the Israelites out of Egyptian bondage. Satan attempted to kill him as soon as he came out of his mother's womb. Matthew 2:13-20 records Herod's attempt to assassinate Jesus, The Son of God, and The Savior of the world. He killed every male child two years old and younger, trying to kill the One Who would give humanity eternal life. Jezebel, the wicked wife of King Ahab, drove the prophet Elijah into hiding in a cave in fear of his life (1Kings 19:1-9). Because he killed her pagan priests (1Kings 18), she threatened to kill him. Ecclesiastes 1:9 tells us that there is nothing new under the sun. Satan has no new tricks. As in the Bible days, he still seeks to thwart the purpose of God by trying to bind and eliminate the people of God.

During my early childhood, I had no idea of what the enemy was doing to me. All I knew was that I was hurt by people that should have protected me. Therefore, I chose to hurt others in order to get revenge. At seven, I was molested by an old man. Then, it seemed I became a target for every pervert in America. At nine years old, I was as developed as a thirteen year old. My brother began molesting me regularly, and my uncle had a fascination with my breasts. By eleven, I was sexually active.

My parents were born in the South, and every spring, winter, and summer break was spent in Newberry, South Carolina. Alcohol was everywhere. My aunts and uncles on Mama's side drank, but Daddy's people drank liquor like it was water.

Newberry was always fun for me because I got together with cousins on both sides of the family, and mischief could have been my middle name back then. I was always the one who came up with wild schemes and I could get anybody to follow me.

My sister, born before my parents were married, had a trailer down there. Although I was a city girl, I became every bit of country as soon as I hit that red dirt down home. We would race each other back and forth around the house, and I would cheat by either cutting through the back or the front door of the trailer. One hot day, in the process of cutting through the house, I got real thirsty. My family would drink liquor in those clear plastic cups and since I was dying of thirst, I took a cup off the table and guzzled down what I thought was water, not even pausing to take a breath. As I drained the cup and started back outside, my chest was on fire! I started choking and coughing, and everyone wanted to know if I were alright.

"Chile' what wrong wit' chu?" Why you carrin' on like that?" my sister asked.

"I thought I was drinkin' water and I done drunk some whiskey!" I said, still coughing. Somebody finally ran and got me some water and I was fine for a while. An hour or so later, I was really feeling alright! I was as high as a kite, and it felt good. Addiction began that day.

From that day on, every chance I got, I would go around sipping drinks left on the tables. People would put their drinks down to go to the bathroom or to get something to eat, and I'd tap their drinks. No one had a clue to what I was doing or why I was acting so strangely all of a sudden. I absolutely loved the feeling I got from those sips, and I wanted more and more.

Once we got back to the city, I began seeking ways to feel good. By now, we had moved to 784 Fox Street, where the torment at night began to manifest in the daytime. There was a period during that time when everyone outside of my home looked like a monster to me. Each person I saw appeared grotesque. I tried to explain this to Mama, but since she didn't see what I saw, she thought I was just acting silly. This kind of stuff began happening to me wherever I went, even down south. It was there that I realized that when I took a few sips from somebody's booze that I didn't see strange stuff at night. So, when I got back to New York, I started looking for booze.

My sister and Ressie weren't around as much because they had their own place, but they'd still come over. My brother got lost in his own world, and I was happy that he did. He didn't "mess" with me as much. I still felt unloved, but I hid it. Whenever I could, I'd sneak into my big brother's room, look at his dirty books, and smoke his cigarette butts. But, none of that stopped the nightmares. It made them grow worse, and I desperately wanted a few sips to make the torture stop.

We didn't stay on Fox Street long. We moved pretty quickly to Clinton Avenue. Daddy was home on rare occasions and Mama would cook great, big meals. She cooked like that all the time, even with her working all the time. My brother started letting me hang out with him on the block. He was already a little gangster. He got high off of all kinds of stuff and he'd let me try whatever he had. He taught me the street game, and I soon became a pro. I learned how to smoke weed (marijuana), pick pockets, and hustle people out of money. At thirteen, my brother had guns in the house. Normally, I'd never tell on him, but the guns scared me. I told him to get rid of them or I'd tell. He had become my world. Ressie had moved to Ohio, which I took very hard, and I didn't have anybody else. My brother was all I knew and I didn't want him to get hurt. The boys he hung out with were dangerous and I tried to persuade my brother to stop hanging with them, but he wouldn't listen. Pretty soon, he was in trouble with the law.

He was sent to Spotford House, a youth detention center in The Bronx, and I completely lost it! I could not stand the fact that my brother was behind bars. I went totally nuts. I knew by now where to get drugs because my brother had introduced me to everybody I needed to know. I smoked weed and drank hard liquor every day. My first drink down south wasn't whiskey. It was corn liquor, so I couldn't drink wine. I drank vodka, scotch, and Southern Comfort, but Jack Daniels was my favorite. Mama had no idea what was happening to me. I began to sass her and totally disrespect her, and I began to rebel.

1Samuel 15:23 says that **"REBELLION IS AS THE SIN OF WITCHCRAFT"**. As I previously mentioned, once Satan gets an entrance, he will build on it. Rejection led to low self-esteem. Low self-esteem allowed hatred and bitterness to come in. Hatred and bitterness opened the door to jealousy and violence. Abuse caused rage. Alcohol was conveniently waiting for me, which led to addiction, and addiction opened the door to out and out rebellion. Satan had me trapped in the spell of witchcraft, and the life my mother had planned for me was fading away, slowly but surely.

# CHAPTER FIVE: TEENAGE WITCH

*"(S)he observed times, and used enchantments, and used witchcraft, and dealt with a familiar spirit, and with wizards"*
*2Chronicles 33: 6b*

I love my mother. I use to tell people that Mama was born saved because she never did anything wrong. She never smoked, drank, and she didn't curse. She tried to curse on occasion but the words never sounded right coming from her. She and I have always been close. She spoiled me and let me do just about anything I wanted to do. I was so smart in school that I got honors every marking period. Mama was so proud of me and she bragged about me to anyone who would listen. God blessed me with a singing voice. I sang all the time around the house, in church, for my friends, in school. I sang anytime and anywhere I could. I was a big show off. The demon of low self-esteem loved this one. It made way for pride.

Because Mama made such a big deal out of me, I thought I was a big deal. I was rude and nasty to people, but never around Mama. When people tried to tell her what I was doing, I'd put on my innocent baby act, and she'd believe me every time. I guess she needed to believe that one of her children would grow up and make something out of themselves.

We moved again, this time to Sedgwick Houses on 174th Street and University Avenue. We had finally made it to the projects. Mama had applied years before and it came through at a time when we really needed it. Mama thought it would help my brother get a new start if we got out of the old neighborhood. But it only got worse – for him and for me. But, now I realize, especially for my Mama. How awful it must be to watch all five of your children throw their lives down the drain. My mother did the best that she could. The horrible events in my past, and the choices I made because of them, were in no way the fault of my mother. She planted the seed of the gospel in me at a very young age, and I rejected it. I thank God daily for my Ma, and there will never be anyone that could ever take her place.

Mama struggled to make ends meet, and all I ever did was make life harder for her. Oh, I cooked, and kept the house clean, but in school, I was a humdinger! I was an A student, but a trouble-maker. A smart mouthed kid who was really a scaredy-cat on the inside. I just acted hard on the outside. At thirteen, I was an alcoholic, a pothead, and a whore. I was also dangerous to mess with back then. I couldn't stand correction – I'd snap out. Mama would be so embarrassed, but that old devil in me only made me act worse because of it. The voices would say, "Since she's embarrassed by you, give her something to really be embarrassed about" – and I did.

We went to church everyday – and I do mean every day. On Sundays, we'd stay all day. The funny thing about my dirty life was this: the people I hung out with the most were all people from my church. My main sex partners at fourteen were the older, married men in the church. I began snorting cocaine around then, and I'd put it in my cigarettes and smoke it, too. Of course, Mama knew nothing of my double life. I was very deceitful and manipulative. I hustled dope left and right – in school and in church – and I never got caught by the police or my Mama.

My singing was at its peak back then, and I taught myself how to play the piano and the organ. I got A's in Spanish class. I was so good I tutored some Spanish speaking students. I was also an avid reader. Any kind of book fascinated me – history, mythology, science, classical literature like Shakespeare, even architecture. I had so much knowledge about foreign lands and cultures that it amazed my teachers, friends, and my family. Even in the clutches of Satan, God was still in the midst of my chaos. I believe all that reading and all that knowledge was preparation for my divine purpose in God today.

At age fifteen, something very strange began to happen to me. I started practicing yoga. I'd sit Indian-style on the floor of my room and I'd meditate. On what, I still don't know up until this day, but I'd sit on that floor for what seemed like hours. Where I got this from I don't know because no one I knew practiced this. I must have read about it or something. I'd go so deep inside myself that I'd have to be called back to reality. My sister, the second from the oldest of my Mama's kids, was around a lot back then. She'd have to carefully pull me back because she said I once came out of a trance violently fighting and cursing.

I always meditated after getting high. Once following a sitting, I heard what I referred to as "the spirit" tell me to erect an altar, and I did. I associated with a few people who burned the candles with the saints on them and I was familiar with the stores that carried them. I went and bought candles, flowers, and incense. I'd open my Bible to a different scripture daily, light a candle and some incense, and "pray to the spirit".

Now, please hear me. I had no idea that I was practicing witchcraft, but I was. The first commandment given to mankind from God is **"THOU SHALT HAVE NO OTHER GODS BEFORE ME"**. The second one is **"THOU SHALT NOT MAKE ANY GRAVEN IMAGE, OR ANY LIKENESS OF ANYTHING THAT IS IN HEAVEN ABOVE, OR IN THE EARTH , OR IN THE WATER; THOU SHALT NOT BOW DOWN TO THEM, NOR SERVE THEM"**(Exodus 20:3-5). All of the candles I used had pictures of "saint-somebody" on them. I prayed to them, I prayed to the spirit, but I never prayed to God in the Name of Jesus. Therefore, "the spirit" that I heard was a demonic familiar spirit. I would ask the spirit things like should I do this or that, and I'd wait for a response. Whatever I was told to do, I obeyed. Some things I did at the spirit's command were against the law. People began coming to me to inquire from the spirit about their personal lives. Whatever I told them, they'd listen. I occasionally had some come back and tell me of horrible things that happened to them because they chose not to take my advice.

Reader, let me share something with you. Nothing that has happened to you in your past was by coincidence or chance. You are a spirit being in a fleshly body, and everything about you and around you is spiritual, whether you realize it or not. God created us to have dominion in the earth (Genesis1:27-28), but Satan's plan is to incapacitate us. He seeks to snatch our power and authority in the earth realm, so he begins his attack against us sometimes even in the womb. Every obstacle you've ever faced, every attack you've ever endured, every trial you've ever encountered, and every trauma that has ever stigmatized you were all designed to keep you from walking in God's intended purpose for your life. But, thank God that what the devil means for harm, God always turns it around for our good. Because of my God-ordained purpose, Satan tried everything he could to stop me from knowing who I really am. Presently, I am delivered from Satan's clutches, and my purpose is to expose his diabolical plots. But

I could never have been as effective as I am today without the knowledge and the experiences of my past.

In no way am I glorifying my past. Sin is an abomination to God, and I believe that I was the biggest sinner there ever was. But if God can forgive me, He can do the same for you. God loves the sinner; He just hates the sin. It doesn't matter if you are or have been a junkie, a crack head, a murderer, a pedophile, a prostitute, a homosexual or a lesbian, a witch or a cult member. If you confess your sins unto God, He is faithful and just to forgive you from **ALL** your sins and clean you from all unrighteousness (1John 1:9).

# PART TWO: THE ADDICTION BEGINS

# CHAPTER ONE: SOLD OUT TO SATAN

*"For we know that the law is spiritual: but I am carnal, sold under sin. For that which I do I allow not: for what I would, that do I not; but what I hate, that do I"*
Romans 7:14-15

I use to say that I was once a drug addict. That was before I understood that the drug addiction was only an outward manifestation of my addiction to the things of this world. 1John 2:16 tells us that the lust of the flesh, the lust of the eyes, and the pride of life are worldly things, and I was addicted to them all.

Although my first sexual encounter was painful, Satan soon sent someone along to get me hooked on sex. That man was my son's father, and I thought he was the finest thing I had ever seen! He looked good, always smelled good, and always knew all the right things to say. He was my brother's friend, and he took his time in courting me. He knew I was scared of sex, so he didn't just jump right on me. He took time to find out what made me tick. He studied me. He came to church with me, complimented me all the time, called me on the phone and we'd talk for hours, and bought me candy, clothes, and even roses. He made a very big fuss out of me, and he supplied me with all the drugs I wanted. I met him at thirteen, and he was the one who turned me out. I was now not only addicted to cocaine but also to sex and money.

In the beginning, I would only have sex for money. My brother and my boyfriend were dealing cocaine for some Italians and I soon learned that I could make a whole lot of money selling my body. Just to take me out to dinner would cost $100. I didn't start out cheap. I prided myself on being a "high class 'hoe". Little did I know what Satan had in store for me.

The places I went and the people I knew were all expensive. I had no business being with any of those people but anything goes in New York. All you need is the right amount of money, and you can get whatever you want. Because of the people I knew, I was able to get in bars and nightclubs in which I sold drugs and myself regularly. I was usually high all of the time. Because I'd always have drugs and money, I had a lot of friends. Friends that used me for my money, drugs, or my body. Friends that corrupted me and helped to make me a child of the devil. Friends that were twice my age, who showed me how to perform sex acts that bought me more tricks. Friends that introduced me to orgies. Friends that turned me on to pills – uppers, downers. I popped pills like I was eating sunflower seeds. I was spaced out all the time, yet I remained in full control of myself and any situation I encountered.

I was also a thief. I really had no reason to steal; I just got a rush out of scaring the heck out of people. I began to party a lot. Hard. My mother was no longer able to control me. I did whatever I wanted anytime I felt like it. I got into fights a lot because of my size. I was maybe one hundred pounds, and some people thought I'd be an easy target. Big mistake. Drugs, alcohol, and demons gave me supernatural strength. The inhumane way I use to beat up on people makes me shudder when I think about it today. I would fight until I drew blood, and still I'd continue hitting my victim.

Although I was ruthless in the streets, I was a punk at home. I never once told my mother or anybody else what was happening to me. My sister began introducing me to her friends and I started sleeping with them for money. I felt bad about how I was living but I still kept doing what I was doing. I was very smart in school, while at the same time, I was dumb. I got straight A's in school but I felt like trash. I was even in all the school plays and talent shows. All of my teachers thought I was this great girl, and none of them believed what all the kids were saying about me. The kids would call me a whore and a tramp, and pretty soon, I was embarrassed to come to school. That's when my life began to unwind.

I was like two people. To my Mama, my teachers, and to the older ladies of my church, I was this little angel destined for greatness in God. To my street friends, I was this ruthless, dangerous, crazy little girl who'd do anything to get what I wanted. No one knew that all the time there were these voices telling me what to do. My altar was where I'd commune with "the spirit". It was there that I'd cry and release all the secrets I held – stuff about my past – the bathroom thing – the things my brother was doing to me that he'd kill me for if I ever told – the older men at church who kept trying to get me in bed with them. Something inside me kept telling me I could never tell. I was convinced that if I told, I'd die. Because I had opened myself up to satanic forces, the devil had complete control over me and I bought all of his lies.

My brother was a master at manipulation. He had me convinced that what he was doing to me was only because he loved me, and that I was so beautiful he couldn't resist himself. Once we moved to University Avenue, he never touched me again, but he began to pervert me in another way. He always had "this dude" he wanted me to meet, and I'd always end up in bed with him.

Once I got saved, it took me a long time to forgive him for pimping me out to his friends. But, God helped me to understand that he, too, was under Satan's control. I had to forgive him in order to receive forgiveness.

During this time, my older brother began to act strange. He's ten years older than me, so he was able to work and help Mama out with the bills. But he refused to work. My other brother was now in jail, and Mama was really struggling. My big brother came up with a plan.

"Yo', Cheryl, if I act like I'm crazy or somethin', Ma won't make me get no job", he said to me one day.

"You better cut that stuff out!" I said. "You keep on actin' like you crazy an' pretty soon, that's what you gonna' be!"

And, sure enough, he went crazy.

The doctors called it schizophrenia. I knew nothing about all of that. All I knew was that it looked like my brother was going insane and it almost drove me insane, too.

# CHAPTER TWO: TOO FAR GONE

*"The way of the wicked is as darkness: they know not at what they stumble"* --- Proverbs 4:19

You have to understand. Even though my family was dysfunctional, they were still my family, and I loved them, each and every one of them. I was always very naïve as a child, and I believed whatever I was told. When circumstances occurred that were contrary to what I believed, I went into a whirlwind of confusion.

My big brother was always the coolest guy I knew. His room was always immaculate; his afro was always trimmed nice and neat; and his style of clothes always made him look like he came out of a fashion magazine. He was always neat and well dressed. Though he smoked marijuana, he was never obnoxious or out of control around me. He and I used to smoke weed together and it was always fun spending time with him. He would always tell me that I was better than what I was doing. He called me a star. He would try and stop me from doing the things I was doing, telling me I needed to make something of myself.

I'll never forget the care and concern in his voice when he'd talk to me. It was real, and it always made me cry.

He was also a ladies man. Women were infatuated with him and there was always a call from "some girl" for him. He was into hats and he had a hat to match every outfit he wore. He had all the latest music and he'd sing and dance like he was one of The Temptations! He was also an awesome basketball player. We called him "Earl the Pearl" and we all hoped he would one day make it to the pro's.

I didn't know how or why he became sick. All I knew was that his illness became my nightmare. No one really knew why he started behaving so strangely at first. Mama took him to the doctors after he began talking to himself. He'd laugh as if there were a person holding a conversation with him. They gave him medication but he wouldn't take it. He would say there was nothing wrong with him. One minute he'd be okay, and in the twinkling of an eye he'd become violent. He stopped bathing and would be missing for weeks. When we'd see him again, he'd looked like a homeless person. He would sleep in the hallways of our apartment building until the police were called. It made me so angry because they'd never hospitalize him and give him treatment. They'd lock him up in jail for vagrancy. Jail only made him worse and all of this was driving me crazy.

To see someone I loved so much suffer the way my brother did hurt me like no pain I've ever known. Sometimes he'd know who I was, and other times he wouldn't. It was one of the most horrible times of my life. I wanted to help him so badly and I tried everything I could. But he'd turn on me and try to hurt me. I soon became afraid of him and he seemed to enjoy making me scared.

My drug usage escalated tremendously during this time. I stayed spaced out so as not to feel the reality of my circumstances. Parties, men, and drugs were all I wanted to focus on.

I thank God for my Mama. Even though I tried to be grown, she still knew how to knock me right back to my senses. She was very persistent about me going to school and to church. Church was Mama's only outlet. On the days she had to work, she always made sure someone picked me up for church. I was actually glad because I loved church for a while. I began playing the piano at eleven and by thirteen, I was getting paid to play for all of the services. I was kind of glad to go to church. Most Sundays were spent in church. We'd take food to church and have dinner after the first service. Then, we'd have a four o'clock service, and most times a seven-thirty service, too. It was usually twelve or one o'clock in the morning when we got home.

Soon, this became a drag because I was strung out on cocaine and marijuana. I was snorting at least a gram of coke every morning before I left my house to go to school. That was just to get me going. On the way to school, I'd smoke a joint. At lunchtime, I usually hung out with a group of girls and we'd smoke a bag of weed. All I did all day was smoke, sniff, and drink. Being in church all day without any drugs would mess me up, so I started bringing my drugs with me.

I am eternally grateful for God's grace and mercy because I was responsible for giving many people their first high.

I had a lot of friends in church back then. They all knew that as soon as church was over, they could get high with me for free. We'd lie and say we were going for a walk or to the store just so we could get high. I had a few friends who lived nearby the church. We'd go to their house, get blasted, go back to church as high as a kite and laugh at every little thing.

My Mama would be so embarrassed but I was too far gone into myself to care. People who cared about me scolded me, telling me to consider what I was doing to my Mama, but I turned a deaf ear to them. I was still meditating, still hearing voices, and still seeing monsters at night. The drugs helped me. They made the monsters go away. They made the pain of life go away. They made me stop feeling the torture that seemed to consume me at times. No one understood when I'd try and explain what I felt, and that made my frustration even greater. I was too far gone.

# CHAPTER THREE: SATAN'S SECRET AGENT

*"For such are false apostles, deceitful workers, transforming themselves into the apostles of Christ"*---2Corinthians 11:13

What I didn't know back then was that the devil had targeted me for destruction. He was on an assignment to kill me, and for a long time I was a walking dead girl. Satan had a secret agent - a boy I now wish I'd never met.

I met him at fifteen, right after my son's father went to jail. Right after I was raped. The rape was horrendous because nobody believed me. The date was May 15th, 1982. I'll never forget it. I was out of Bamboo, the paper used to roll marijuana. It was a warm night so I ran out to the store in a pair of skin tight shorts. There was an abandoned building right outside the projects that we lived in. I didn't think for a second that anyone was going to mess with me. How wrong I was. A man jumped out and snatched me in the building.

I cannot describe my fear. I was that little girl in the bathroom again. This time was worse because the man had a gun and a mask. When I got back in the house, I felt dirty and nasty. I immediately took off my shorts. They were still intact because he actually made me take them off and put them back on. I took off my blouse and I just sat in the bathtub with the shower running. I was still there when my mother came home. She came in and got me because she got no response from me after calling my name several times. I was just sitting there, in shock. That was the day I stopped crying.

I tried to tell her what happened but I started to hyper-ventilate. Once I finally got it out, she took me to the hospital and the police were called. This was also the day that I began hating cops. They berated me with stupid questions, insinuating that I somehow got what I deserved. "You shouldn't have been outside half dressed" one officer told me. Because I wasn't crying, they accused me of lying. They told me to confess that I was just with some boy and to stop trying to hide it from my Mama. I began yelling all kinds of obscenities at them as my Mama was dragging me out of there. I soon had to get a grip of myself because I realized that I was in a lot of pain. The doctors had given me a shot in each thigh that prevented sexually transmitted diseases.

The devil had a field day with this one. I began having more nightmares but now, the monsters were raping me. I slept with a gun under my pillow and I carried it everywhere I went, even to church. I was too proud to act like I was hurting or scared around anyone, so nobody suspected a thing. But the devil knew. That's when he sent his secret agent.

It was May 27$^{th}$. I remember the date because it was the day before his birthday. I'd known him from school. He was as black as midnight, but as charming as a rattlesnake. We got together for his birthday and had a good time. We began seeing each other on a daily basis and he played on me. He got me to open up and talk to him about my pain. I told him how hurt I was over my boyfriend going to jail, how it pained me to see my brother in the shape he was in, and I also told him about the rape. He acted as if it had happened to his own mother. He cried and cried and cried – and that's what got me into bed with him.

I thought I was in love. This boy became my everything. He was very romantic and he gave me all of his attention. I began cutting classes to be with him, and I stopped sleeping with other people and selling drugs. He became my sole supplier of drugs. The money I made in church I gave to him, and I did whatever he told me to do. I was so grateful to have somebody make me the center of their world that I did whatever I could to please him, even go against my family.

At seventeen, he moved me out of my Mama's house. My brother had gotten very violent and he and I fought all the time. My sister would leave her daughter with me for days at a time and he didn't like this. It interrupted our time together. He also knew that my sister would fix me up with men, and he called himself "rescuing" me from all of that. I was so deceived by him that I truly believed that this was the best thing to do. My mother always defended my brother, saying he was sick, and this angered me. He once tried to throw me out of our twelve story apartment window, and I was supposed to overlook that. My father tried to intervene once or twice, but it made no difference. I hated him. He'd left us when I was ten years old. I didn't have any respect for him, and I certainly didn't believe him when he said my brother wasn't going to hurt me anymore. How was he going to stop him!

So, I packed up all of my clothes, and I left home at seventeen years old.

# CHAPTER FOUR: DEVIL IN DISGUISE

*"And no marvel: for Satan himself is transformed into an angel of light"* --- 2Corinthians 11: 14

I really thought I had it going on! I was seventeen, slim, and shapely; I was the head cashier at C-Town Supermarkets; I had a man who loved me, and nobody could tell me anything. I stopped going to school altogether and I became a housewife.

Wow. I really believed back then that I was a housewife, but the truth is I was just a little girl caught up in a grown woman's situation.

Our apartment was a shambles when we moved in, but two weeks later it was ready to be featured in Homes and Gardens. I never had to spend my money on anything but me. He wouldn't let me. He worked for LaGuardia Airport and sold cocaine, so he made plenty of money. He paid for everything, from toilet paper to every utility bill. He was sweet and loving to me all the time and everyone loved him. He always bought gifts for Mama, and he'd visit her without my knowledge. He, my sister, and one of my older brothers became as thick as thieves. I'd work all day and they'd be in my apartment, partying and getting high. He worked nights so we were only together for a few hours a day and on Saturdays. I was still going to church on Sundays.

I consistently thank God for gifting me to play the piano. It kept me going to church back then. Mama was the Sunday School Superintendent, so she knew the Scriptures quite well. She'd always come up with a question that none of us kids could answer and it infuriated me. So, I began to study The Bible just so I could outsmart my Mama. Even though the devil thought he had me, God was planting a seed in me that is still producing a harvest even now.

I would study The Bible for hours. Even though I worked, I still had a lot of time to myself. My boyfriend didn't like for me to have company and I obeyed whatever he asked. I'd get high and read The Bible. The more I read, the more I wanted to read. Although I didn't understand it, I memorized passages of Scripture. I also read books on Greek mythology, Hinduism, Buddhism, poetry, science fiction, astrology, and various cults around the world. I studied Amish and Irish history, and the gods of different cultures. I was fascinated with Chinese and Japanese architecture. I read all the latest romance novels and every book ever written by Stephen King. I couldn't stop reading.

I'd try and share the vast amount of knowledge I acquired from reading with my boyfriend, and he would become furious, especially when I mentioned God or The Bible to him. He'd say it was bad enough that I went to church. He wouldn't stand for me quoting Scripture to him. He worked from eleven at night until seven in the morning. At first, he had no problem with me working the morning shift. Then, he began complaining that I was never home with him. So, I began working part time. For about a month or so he'd be home when I came in, but then he started coming in at six and seven in the evening. Whenever I questioned him about it, he'd explode and violently curse at me. I wanted to know what he was doing all day, so I quit my job to be at home more with him. It was one of the stupidest decisions I ever made.

All day long, all we did was snort cocaine. Lots of it. I got a kick out of putting cocaine in my mouth because I loved the numb feeling I got from it. I had found out that packing my cigarettes with cocaine brought an instant rush, so I'd make "koolies" by the pack. There was nothing like the high I got from those cigarettes. I'd smoke coke in marijuana at times but I enjoyed the koolies more. I began to snort less and less because my nose began to bleed profusely when I did. I had a couple of friends that I was allowed to hang out with on the block. Mostly, I was with my boyfriend's sister. That way, he could keep tabs on me. He had girlfriends everywhere, but I didn't know it just yet. I found out quickly enough, and I decided to get even.

# CHAPTER FIVE:
# THE NIGHTMARE BEGINS

*"I sink in deep mire, where there is no standing:
I am come into deep waters,
where the floods overflow me"*
Psalms 69: 2

I will probably remember this day as long as I live because it changed who I was. I had just come home from the store. I put my key in the lock and tried to open the door but it was chained from the inside. It took a few minutes for him to open the door, and I was outraged. When he finally let me in, I went into our bedroom to find some dirty looking girl with her two dirty looking kids on my bed! Somebody should have told her about me before she pulled such a stupid stunt. I behaved so badly that the girl almost left her kids in my house trying to get away from me.

That was the first day that I saw the devil in his eyes. He grabbed me by my shoulders and shook me. The look on his face was so evil, it scared me. He didn't hit me, but his presence was so forceful. The way I felt at that moment was the same way I felt whenever the monsters appeared to me. It was eerie. I felt their presence but I didn't see them; I saw him.

Life was never the same again from that moment on. I wasn't the type of girl you could cheat on and get away with it. So, I began to have an affair with one of the most understanding men I had ever met. He was much older and had been trying to date me for years. He wasn't cute, but he was very charming. He was flirty and romantic, something my boyfriend stopped being months ago. I didn't sleep with him right away, though. I was trying to give my boyfriend a chance to make things right with us. He had started missing work, but he still wasn't coming home. When he was there, he wouldn't have sex with me, and I didn't understand why.

I would do everything I could to arouse him but it was all to no avail. Now, remember; I was a sex addict and had been one for years. I reminded him of this for two months. Each time I pleaded with him to do something to fix our relationship, he'd become rude and obnoxious and storm out of the house. I couldn't understand how the nice, sweet, and gentle man I had moved in with had turned into one of my nightmare monsters.

I should have left him then. Why didn't I just leave? Because he was a master at seduction. He sensed when I was about to leave him and he'd always come up with something to win me over. He'd go out and by me some expensive, exquisite gift, tell me how much he loved and needed me, and how he couldn't stand to be without me. And I'd fall for it every time. But through all of this, he would not or could not have sex with me.

One day, I watched him out of the living room window as he went into that girl's house – the one I caught in my house. I sat on my stoop for two hours, watching to see when he'd come out. I was supposed to be someplace else, but I had changed my mind and decided to stay on that stoop until he came out. As I waited, I smoked a couple of joints and drank a few beers, wondering what excuse he'd come up with. When he finally came down, I acted as if I never knew where he was. I smelled the girl on him. He didn't even have the decency to shower. He said he had been with his boys. He didn't know I was watching because I hid behind the bushes in front of our house. He lied so nicely, and I never let on that I knew.

That night, I went to my friend, and I continued to go as often as I could for months.

His mother was the first to suspect something was going on. She and I never liked each other, but we tolerated one another. There was something evil about her, and she had too much control over her son. His father was very abusive to her and that probably had a lot to do with her behavior. We use to get high together occasionally and we'd sit up until two or three in the morning. When I broke the routine, she started asking questions. Of course I'd lie, but she wouldn't let up and she told her son.

I still can't believe how dumb and stupid I was back then. That boy had some kind of spell on me. I told my friend that I couldn't keep seeing him, that I felt guilty and that I was going to tell my boyfriend about the whole thing. He said that it was a bad idea and that I should not, under any circumstances, tell my boyfriend about us. He said it would be the worst thing I could ever do, but I didn't believe him. I thought he'd understand, so I went home and told the truth.

I had on a pair of Casals, an expensive pair of glasses that he'd brought me. I was crying, something I didn't normally do. He was that calm, loving person he was the night I told him about the rape. He kept assuring me that he would understand, that I could trust him with anything, and like a fool, I believed him. After I'd told him the whole story, he took off my glasses. I thought he was going to hug me and wipe away my tears because he was saying, "It's alright, Baby Doll. I still love you".

But he hit me. Over and over again. He punched me, kicked me, spit on me, and threw me all across the room. He was crying and screaming, "How could you do this to me? I have been so good to you! I took you from your family, who treated you like dirt, and I gave you everything you could ever want, and this is the thanks I get! This is how you treat me?! Well, after tonight, you'll never get the chance to do it again!"

Something in me – no – everything in me died that night. I felt so ashamed and guilty. He kept saying I deserved the beating I was getting and I believed him. He also said I deserved to die for what I'd done, and I believed that, too. That night, he tried to kill me by choking me to death. What made him stop could have only been the angels of God.

Satan really had a field day with this one. He had been trying to make me feel worthless for years, and he had finally succeeded. I sank into a pit of hopelessness and despair. I believed that I was evil and that I needed to be punished. That night, he beat me until I looked like the Elephant Man. Later on, he tried to hang himself in our bathroom and swore if I ever left him, he'd kill himself.

It was the first night of what would become my worst nightmare.

# PART THREE: AND THEN THERE WAS CRACK

# CHAPTER ONE: UNHOLY DESIRES

*"Wherein in time past we walked according to the course of this world, according to the prince of the power of the air, the spirit that now worketh in the children of disobedience:*
*Among whom also we had our conversation in times past in the lusts of our flesh, fulfilling the desires of the flesh and of the mind; and were by nature the children of wrath, even as others"* ---
*Ephesians 2: 2-3*

I learned how to hide my bruises. He learned how to bruise me in places that people couldn't see. He got high more than a lot now. He began cooking cocaine with baking soda and water in a glass beaker. He wouldn't tell me why at first, so I started asking some people that I knew. Eventually, I found out that he was selling crack. I wondered to myself "what in the world is crack?"

The streets of The Bronx were in a frenzy over these little rocks. The rocks were sold in little clear vials with red, blue, yellow, orange, or green tops. There were empty vials all over the streets. Once, I came in our kitchen and he was bottling these little vials with crack. He was upset that I had come in but it was too late to try and hide it. He had a crack pipe on the table and I wanted to know how to use it, so I persuaded him to show me. He put the little rock in the bowl, lit a lighter and put it to the rock, and pulled on the stem. The bowl filled up with smoke and that was all to it. Seeing it was not good enough for me; I wanted to try it. He resisted a bit, but I finally won, and I took my first hit.

It was like my mind and my body separated. I was no longer aware of anything else. All I knew was that I wanted more. He had to go out and make his money, so I was left at home. Usually, I bagged up his cocaine for him, so he trusted me to bottle up some vials. There were twenty vials, valued at twenty dollars a piece. Plus, he left me two vials for myself. He left about 11:30 that morning, and by the time he got back at 7:30 that night, I was down to half a vial. I smoked over $400 worth of cocaine all by myself.

That was in January of 1985. I was 17 years old.

It is my belief that crack cocaine was inspired by Satan himself. It is the most destructive drug that I have ever known. To ingest this drug is equivalent to swallowing several demons. It controls the mind because it births another spirit into a person. Heroin is a demonic drug also, which can cause a person to have severe dysfunctions in the body if the drug is not administered to them. It can even cause death in some cases because the body becomes dependent on the drug. Crack is a mind drug. You will not go into cardiac arrest if you do not have a hit of crack. But the drug can make you think that you will.

In retrospect, I now know that it was the voice of the devil that completely controlled my every waking thought, and even my dreams, after that first hit. My boyfriend couldn't believe that I smoked all that dope, and he was afraid to leave me alone. I didn't know why at that time, nor did I care. All I wanted to do was get another hit.

From that day on, I no longer wasted my coke by snorting it up my nose. I cooked it and smoked every grain I got my hands on. I no longer wanted my favorite drink, Jack Daniels, nor did I care to smoke weed. Crack had taken complete control over my life. Any kind of emotion I had died the moment I took my first hit. Feelings of care, concern, or consideration for anybody or anything besides crack became non-existent in me. There were a few brief moments when the crack demon lifted, and I was allowed to feel remorse and guilt. But those feelings only made me seek more crack, in order to escape the reality of what I had become.

That March, I turned 18, and I left the church all together. I was completely consumed by crack cocaine. I lied to Mama about needing money for bills or food, just so I could get money for crack. When all other avenues of getting money were exhausted, I went back to my old trade of prostitution in order to get money to buy drugs. My boyfriend was strung out by now also, so he no longer disputed with me about sleeping with other men. He encouraged me to turn tricks so we could have money to get high. He couldn't sell anymore because every ounce he got, we smoked. My sister was a part of this also, and our apartment soon became a crack house where anything went on, all in the name of getting high.

There were still the fights he and I had – big, ugly ones. Due to crack usage and those fights, I was one horrible, looking mess. I no longer did my hair or my nails, which I had always been so meticulous about. I only bathed because I didn't want to lose customers because of my smell. Sleep came only after my body was completely exhausted after days of exertion.

We sold everything worth selling back then – TV's, irons, clothes, shoes, jewelry, and kitchen appliances from eating and cooking utensils to microwave ovens. Whatever we could sell, whatever we could do, including stealing from our parents, we did in order to feed our addiction.

How could a person debase themselves so, with no feelings of remorse or regret about anything or anybody?

How could a person lie and steal from their own mother, just to get high?

How could a person go into a clothing store, try on clothes and walk out the store, with no fear of being caught by the police, just so they could sell the clothes in order to get high?

Insanity. Absolute insanity.

# CHAPTER TWO: INSANITY

*"And He (Jesus) asked him,
'What is thy name?' And he answered, saying,
'Legion: for we are many'"*
*Mark 5:9*

The Webster's Dictionary definition of the word ***"insanity"*** is ***"to be deranged in mind or intellect; to be senseless; to be a lunatic"***. In the Gospel of Matthew 17: 14-21, there is a story of a man who brings his son to Jesus because he is a lunatic. **My personal definition of *"insanity"* is *"to be a crack addict"*.**

Everyone I knew and loved no longer mattered to me anymore. I had lost sense of time, so day and night intertwined with each other. Most of the time, I didn't know where I was, and occasionally, I forgot who I was. My boyfriend and I began to drift apart. I was more concerned about getting high than I was about a relationship. Besides, I was getting tired of the fights. We had starting fighting over crack – who got the first hit, and who got the last. What an awfully dumb thing to fight over. I was no longer afraid of him, so I fought back, and like I said before, I fought until I saw blood. Even then, I'd still keep on fighting. Since a black eye made it difficult to pick up "tricks" (men who paid for sex), I tried to get away from him. Many times, it almost cost me my life.

The day I decided to tell him it was over, he beat me so bad that I couldn't walk for two days. My sister just happened to come by that day and she was able to get me out of there. He never tried to fight anyone else but me. He was afraid of my sister and my brothers because they had confronted him about abusing me many times. We took all of my clothes that night, but I had to leave my cat. I told him I'd be back for her in a day or so, and he agreed to take care of her.

Because it took a couple of days for me to move around properly, I didn't go back for my cat until four days later. I had sense enough not to go alone, so I asked Mama to go with me. We lived on the second floor of a small walk up with no hallway, just an apartment on each side of the steps. When I got half way up the steps, I heard my cat crying. I thought she must have known it was me and was waiting at the door for me. As I neared the top step, I saw that she was sitting in her litter box in between the doors of the two apartments. She looked so frightened, and I knew she was freezing because it was about twenty degrees outside that day. That fool was so evil that he'd put my cat outside to freeze to death. I was so angry that I actually screamed to the top of my lungs! When I picked her up, she seemed as if she was hurt, and I realized that he'd probably kicked her around just to get back at me. I loved that cat as if she was my own child and everyone knew it. I kicked and banged on the door, still screaming and cursing, but I got no answer.

If you've been paying attention thus far, you should know that I wasn't going to just let him get away with that one! I had snapped back to my old self for a while. I went back to my mother's house, and that night I devised a plan. The next day, I called him at his apartment and I begged him to take me back. I told him how sorry I was and that I was miserable without him. I laid it on thick, and he fell for it. He let me come back.

I didn't bring too many clothes. I told him that I'd ease my clothes back slowly, so I wouldn't have to explain anything to my mother. Again, I became the "dutiful, obedient little housewife". That's what he called me at times. I played this role for a good week or two. Then, I made my move.

It was a Friday night. He was off that weekend; the house was immaculate and smelled of scented candles. I had a superb dinner waiting for him, slow jams were playing on the radio, and I was well stocked with his favorite drinks and lots of drugs. We stayed up until sometime late on Saturday evening and finally, he fell asleep. I had no intention of sleeping. Once he was asleep, I went to work.

I will not describe how, but that night I issued out "pay back" for the abuses I had received at this man's hands. When I think back to how diabolical it all was, I am appalled. Even though I felt justified at the time, it was a terribly horrible thing to do. When I satisfied my desire for revenge, I walked back home and told Mama to take me to the Port Authority. I left that night to go to Youngstown, Ohio, to stay with my sister and Ressie. I was nineteen years old.

# CHAPTER THREE: RUNNING INTO A TRAP

*"The proud have hid a snare for me, and cords; they have spread a net by the wayside; they have set gins for me"*
*Psalms 140:5*

It was a twelve hour bus ride so I had a lot of time to think. What was happening to me? How had I stooped so low? I thought about the last four years and realized I had sold myself to the devil. I was even a murderer because I had gotten an abortion the year before. I wanted the child, but my boyfriend and his family were totally against me having it. I had allowed myself to be pressured into killing a child. I allowed myself to become a prostitute in order to use crack. I had stolen from my mother and nearly broken her heart. I vowed to myself that I would never use crack again. But even as I said this to myself, I realized that the devil was talking to me. He was telling me that I wasn't going to get away. At that moment, my heart filled with that old familiar fear, my breathing got heavy, and my stomach got that anxious feeling.

Thanks be unto God that I have acquired a lot of knowledge concerning what was taking place in me back then. I have studied books on demonic possession and I have learned that heavy breathing and pressure in the chest and stomach are signs of the presence of a demon. I had opened myself up to witchcraft years ago, and the ingestion of all those drugs had made it easy for Satan to control me. In many satanic practices, drugs are used in order to make a person more susceptible for demons to enter into them. At that moment on the back of that Greyhound bus, the crack demon overtook me. I was sincerely trying not to think about crack, but the taste of it came up in my mouth, my stomach got all nervous as it usually did when I was about to take a hit, and all of a sudden I was right back in the clutches of the devil. I had to have a hit.

For every person reading this who has never experienced the horror of these emotions, stop reading for a moment and take time to **GIVE GOD A PRAISE!**

For those who know firsthand what I am talking about, who have been freed from Satan's clutches, **GIVE GOD A PRAISE**!

For those that are reading who are entangled by Satan's trickery even now, and for those who know someone that is, **GIVE GOD A PRAISE,** because I am proof that **YOU CAN BE DELIVERED FROM CRACK COCAINE!** It is my prayer that the knowledge I have acquired over the years will encourage you to **BELIEVE THAT JESUS CHRIST CAN SET YOU FREE!**

Because I had no one in my life that had experience in how to handle a crack demon, I suffered for years with this addiction. As soon as I got to Ohio, I started snorting cocaine. Of course, I left New York with a heavy supply. It was much easier to transport drugs back then. My oldest sister was a big help to me because she adamantly refused to let me use cocaine. She was my oldest sister and she had this way with me – I was still scared of her! Although I was grown, she'd still go upside my head if she had to, and she promised to if I didn't give up all the drugs that I had in my possession when I got to her house. She was horrified by what crack had done to me. I was probably ninety pounds when she picked me up from the bus station. I thought I could get away with snorting with her because we'd smoked weed together for a few years. I would spend part of the summer with her in Ohio, until I'd moved in with that guy. Since I knew she liked to sniff, I bought extra, thinking that she would be okay with me sniffing, but she wasn't having any of it. She took maybe a half of a gram, and made me flush the rest down the toilet.

For a few weeks, I tried in my own strength to resist smoking cocaine. I quickly got a job in a department store called Hills. I tried so hard to go back to what I had called a normal life. I worked as much as I could, helped my sister with the bills, spent time with my nieces, and tried to stay out of trouble. But Satan wasn't done with me yet. In fact, he had only just begun.

A co-worker asked me to me to go to a club with her and I was raring to go, since it had been a long time since I actually went to a club where there was dancing taking place. For the last two years, I only hung out to smoke crack. I was ready to have some normal fun again.

The club was called The Ringside and it was wild! I was a very good dancer back in those days and being from New York was a plus. The guys thought New York girls were wild and I decided not to disappoint them; I danced with just about every one of them in the club.

All night there was this one particular guy who kept checking me out, but he wouldn't approach me. He was very good looking with a weightlifter's body. I asked my friends who he was but they had never seen him before. He never danced with anyone all night; he just watched me as I danced, and I flirted with him while I danced. But I wasn't going to be the one who made the first move. Normally, I would have, but something about him made me apprehensive. He acted as if he was all that, so I was going to make him come to me. We were almost out of the parking lot when he pulled his car in front of us. He drove an olive green Jaguar, and he asked my name and we exchanged phone numbers. My friends were all psyched that this fine looking guy who obviously had money was trying to get with me, and so was I.

For the next two days all I thought about was him. I didn't know him from Adam, but in my mind we'd already become the best of friends. I was once again smoking weed and drinking occasionally, but I didn't indulge during the week, only on the weekends. Finally, he called and asked me out on a date and I agreed. We went to dinner, a movie, and then back to his place. Bottles of liquor filled the bar he had in his den and he offered me my favorite drink, Jack Daniels. He said he remembered what I drank from the night at the club. He asked did I get high and of course my response was yes. And of course, he had about five grams of cocaine. We got high all night, and he became my new best friend. The devil had me trapped again.

# CHAPTER FOUR: WHEN CRACK CALLS

*"For I delight in the law of God after the inward man: but I see another law in my members, warring against the law of my mind, and bringing me into captivity to the law of sin which is in my members"---Romans 7:22-23*

The next ten years were literally a living hell. I was a walking dead girl most of that time. I stayed in Ohio only a few months more after meeting that guy because I had to get back to New York. Crack was calling me. Before leaving I spent two weeks in jail. I was livid! After all the things I'd done in New York, I'd never been caught, and I get to Ohio, a place hardly anyone I knew from the city had even heard of, and I go to jail for trying to break up a fight! Those two weeks behind bars should have been enough to scare me straight, but it wasn't. I just determined in my mind never to get caught by the police again.

    I was released from jail January 25, 1988, and I was back in The Bronx two days later. My first stop was to the smoke shop to get me a pipe, then to the crack house to get a hit. My family only saw me on the weekends. I'd stay gone during the week, roaming the streets getting high, going from one crack house to another, until Saturday night. I'd come home so I could go to church. I was still a very good musician and the church paid me very well. As soon as church was over, I went on my way to buy crack with the church money.

Sometime during the summer, I found out I was pregnant. I was ecstatic! I'd finally have something I could call my own. Even though I knew what crack could do to my baby, I continued to use. I could not control it. I craved crack like most pregnant women crave pickles and ice cream. I would sit somewhere by myself, hitting on the pipe with tears streaming down my face, afraid for my baby and ashamed of myself, but unable to overcome the power of my addiction.

Many people thought I didn't care about my baby or my family, but that was so far from the truth. Oh! I loved them tremendously, and I was humiliated with myself for what I was doing to them. The demons controlling my mind and my body knew this, and they would attack me with guilt and condemnation.

*"Look at you! You're pathetic! How could you stoop so low? What does your family need you for? You're good for nothing and they hate you, so why don't you just forget about trying to quit? You're useless anyway! Nobody likes you – nobody even cares about you! They're probably all wishing you would just kill yourself and get it over with! You see how they treat you when you come around? They carry their purses around with them so you don't rob them! They don't want you around. Look at how they are looking at you! Just who do they think they are anyway, acting all high and mighty?! They think they're better than you. Why should you have to put up with all that? They keep telling you you're no good, you'll never amount to anything, and you're downright hopeless, so just forget about them! You don't need them! You don't need anybody! Go 'head on and get high!"*

My prayer for you, dear reader, is that you will never know the hell of having to walk around the world with thoughts like these attacking your mind. No matter how I try to explain it, if you've never been addicted in the way that I was, it will be difficult for you to actually understand. Suicide became a constant companion, continuously trying to lure me into the grave. Many attempts were made, but to the glory of God, each one failed. God had his angels protecting me from death and I continue to praise Him for it even now.

My Nadia Nicole was born February 2, 1989, two months before my due date, a premature baby doll weighing only 4 pounds, 13 ounces. I had to have a Caesarian birth because of premature labor, and I was as high as a kite. The doctors knew right away that I was an addict. I was 85 pounds when I got pregnant; when I delivered, I was only 103. My Nadi was the most beautiful baby I had ever seen. She was so tiny, though, and her color was gray for the first few days. Since she wouldn't eat, she had to stay in an incubator, and I couldn't hold her a lot. All I could do was sit beside her and cry, during which time the demons tortured me non-stop. The Children's Services were threatening to take her until Mama intervened. She became her partial guardian and the stipulation was made that I could only be around my baby if Mama was present. I also had to go to counseling and parenting classes, and attend a drug treatment program.

Most normal people would have stopped using, but addicts are far from being considered normal. I was tormented in my mind until I got a hit. Once crack was in my system, the devil controlled my thoughts for days at a time. I didn't care about time, or people, or anything else but crack and how to get money to get it. I truly despise the devil, because there were moments when the demons lifted and I came back to reality, but only to realize that it had been four days since I'd seen my baby. I'd realize that I had left her somewhere that I shouldn't have, and I'd call Mama to go and get her. The disgust in her voice was all the devil needed to send me out on another two or three day binge. It was truly a living nightmare.

Not long after Nadia was born, the man who taught me the ropes in the sex department came back into my life, and he took the role of Nadia's father for a while. For a year or so, my drug use slowed down but not completely. This guy was the reason for it because he made me slow down and be a mother to my daughter. Then, he got into trouble with the law again and went to jail once more, but not until I became pregnant with our son. Again, I began to crave crack cocaine, and it was once again driving me to insanity. Because I was afraid of what the authorities would do to me and my children if this baby was born addicted, I sincerely tried to stop smoking crack. But again, the addiction was too powerful. But, thanks be to God, He protected my baby from his crack-addicted Mama.

My Pierre Hassan was born March 20, 1991, weighing 6 pounds, 10 ounces, miraculously with no trace of cocaine in his system. I realize and acknowledge that "luck" had nothing at all to do with it. Because of the plans that God had for my life, even with me living outside of His Will, He still watched over me, protected me, and even continuously blessed me. For this, I give Him praise!

When I brought my son home, a terrible fear, one that I'd never known before, overcame me. Every fiber of my being instinctively knew that it was time for me to take my children and leave New York. I knew that if I didn't leave immediately, I was going to die. When I told my family this, they all thought that I had finally lost my whole mind. But I hadn't. In the hospital room, as I was in labor, I started to pray. I didn't realize then that God was talking to me. All I knew was that the feeling to leave was strong enough to convince me that it was definitely time for me to go.

On April 10, 1991, I took my two kids and one suitcase full of clothes, got on the Greyhound bus, and moved to Youngstown, Ohio.

# CHAPTER FIVE: CAUGHT AND CONTROLLED

*"When the unclean spirit is gone out of a man, he walketh through dry places, seeking rest; and finding none, he saith, I will return unto my house whence I came out. And when he cometh, he findeth it swept and garnished. Then goeth he, and taketh to him seven other spirits more wicked than himself; and they enter in, and dwell there: and the last state of that man is worse than the first"*
Luke 11:24-27

For the first time in my addict years, I was determined to stay off crack. I became aware of what was happening to me and my kids because of crack, and I made up my mind to quit. I got a job in Ohio, got my own place, and I was okay for two whole years. And just when I thought it was over – **THEN THERE WAS CRACK!**

It was waiting for me. It began surrounding me with people that used it. It was subtle at first and I put up what I called a good fight. But a situation arose where I was ***"emotionally ship-wrecked"***, and the devil took full advantage of it.

Although my son's father went back to jail, we stayed in contact with each other. Actually, I took care of him the whole time he was in prison. I sent him packages of food and clothing every month, making sure he had personal hygiene items as well as money for commissary. We were "in love" and supposed to get married when he came home. I had arranged to be at the prison when he was released. Mama, who had moved to Ohio two months after I did, drove me and the kids all the way to Riker's Island in New York, so we could be there as soon as he walked out of the gate. Pierre was two years old and had never seen his father. This man was no where to be found. We went to his mother's house and she informed us that he'd been released two days prior to our arrival. She apologized to us for her son's inconsideration, but she had no idea where he was. On our way out the building, we met him in the hall, coming in the building all hugged up with some girl.

I was traumatized, devastated, and infuriated. There was a horrible fight in that hallway, and my children were screaming and afraid. I was too mad to cry, and it would be years before I felt any emotion but anger again.

That night, I snuck out of the hotel we were staying in, and stayed gone for two days. I went back to all my old familiar grounds and I got high. This time, it was different. I was aware of my emotions. I felt outraged and humiliated. Here I was, like a stupid fool, believing in a con man that everybody said was using me from the start, and I was too dumb to see it. It turned me into a mean, hateful woman who was only going to think about herself from here on out.

I went back to Ohio and went into full blown addiction all over again, but this time, it was seven times worse. Youngstown is a small town where everybody knows everybody, and I thoroughly embarrassed my entire family. We were all in the same church, where again I was the musician, taking the church money to get high. I was seen by church members walking on Hillman Street, which was called "the hooker's stroll". Everybody in town knew I was leaving my kids home alone, while I was out selling my body to get high. I was the laughingstock of town, and I was afraid of what was happening to me. I didn't want to be a crack-head, but again, I had no control to stop.

The last two years of addiction were the worst for me because I desperately wanted to be free. I'd stay sober for days at a time, and then I'd relapse and go back to using all over again. The one thing that I remember about those days was that I was always extremely tired - tired in my body, tired in my spirit, and tired in my soul. I felt as if I needed to go lay in an open grave somewhere and just let somebody cover me up with dirt. I was dead. I couldn't go forward, I couldn't go backward, and in 1994, I found out that I was once again pregnant.

I was hysterical because I did not want to bring another child into the world while I was still strung out on crack. The father of this child and I were together for about a year or so before I conceived and he was trying to help me stay clean. He was a former addict himself and he played an important part in my recovery, but I certainly put him through hell first. The first four months of the pregnancy I used constantly, hoping to abort the baby. But then, I felt her moving around in me and things changed. My first two children moved in my womb and I bonded with them, but this child's movements inside of me were altogether different. Although I still craved cocaine, I couldn't use like I use to with my other babies. Those two would settle down when I smoked, but this baby acted as if she was trying to claw through my stomach! I was petrified. I had the doctors run all sorts of tests, thinking that because of me, there was something wrong with my baby.

Guilt completely broke me at that point. My tears were still locked up inside of me. I hadn't cried in years. I wanted to cry, but I was buried so deep inside myself that I couldn't. I wanted to be free, but I had no idea how to go about it. Drug programs were of no help to me; I came away from them with a stronger urge to use. Church wasn't working either because I wasn't listening to the preacher. He had never been where I was so he couldn't tell how to come out.

By this time, my family was totally exhausted with trying to help me. Mama and Ressie were the only two who believed that someday I'd be free. Yet, at the same time, they stopped making addiction easy for me. They'd come get the kids and keep them, so I wouldn't neglect taking care of them. I was a horrible mother to Nadi and Pete, but they still loved their Mommy, and they would cry every time I left them. I thank God for Mama and Ressie. They would assure my kids that God was going to heal their Mommy, and we'd all be fine one day. Although it was definitely true back then, never once did I hear them tell my kids that I was a bad mother. Years later, though, my kids told me that when I wasn't around, they talked about me like I was a dog.

I must interject something right here to the family members of the addict. The children of addicts do not understand drug addiction, especially if they are younger children. They only know that, good or bad, they love their parents. Shelter and protect them physically if you must, but do not belittle the addicted parent in the presence of their child(ren). Not all addicts stay addicted. Even if some do not get delivered, it is still wrong to condemn a parent in the presence of their child. The addict suffers from a hell that I pray none of you readers will ever know. Addiction is a sickness, a demonic attack against the people God created in His image. The Word of God teaches us not to judge others in Matthew 7. As bad as an addict can behave, and as much as you may think they deserve spiteful treatment, the addict is a sick, tormented spirit who will spend eternity in hell if he/she does not get delivered. As parents, as spouses, family and friends of the addict, let us first look to God and pray for their deliverance, and also seek to restore the addict and their families into right relationships.

My mother and my niece also stopped giving me money. They knew, no matter what story I came up with, I'd only use it for drugs. I was still welcome in Mama's house, but I couldn't stay very long. The kids could stay as long as they liked, but I had to leave. My family knew that if given half the chance, I'd steal something. My mother stopped putting over-the-counter medicines in the medicine cabinet in her bathroom because I would steal them, too. I had to be followed into every room that I went into. I had become that untrustworthy.

I finally couldn't stand myself any longer, and that Christmas of 1994, I made a promise to my kids to get my act together. Nadia was five, and Pierre was three. We all had a wonderful Christmas. I actually brought them gifts that year, and didn't steal them from under the Christmas tree as I'd done once or twice before. Usually, Mama had to buy them gifts because I spent every dime on drugs. I was truly happy that day, but it only lasted for a little while.

1995 arrived. The entire month of January, I remained drug free. My baby was due March 20, so I was really trying to do right. I was eating healthy, being good to my kids, and doing okay. Nadia's sixth birthday came and went, and still I managed to stay clean. But the devil would not let go that easily.

One day while in the grocery store, I ran into an old friend, one of my old "get high partners". We started to reminisce about old times, and that old familiar spirit re-awakened in me. The anxious jitters in my stomach were aroused by the memory of my last hit. For over a week, I became jittery and restless. I was easily agitated and yelled at the kids for no apparent reason. Mama came by one evening and noticed my behavior.

"Cherie, you ain't foolin' nobody, you know. I know you just tryin' to come up with an excuse to leave this house", she told me. "You can keep on playing around with God if ya' want to, but you gonna' go out there n' get a hold of the wrong stuff, and next thing you know, you gonna' be hearin' voices just like your brother. You can't just keep on playing with

God like that, Chile'. He got a call on your life n' He ain't gonna' let you keep on getting' 'way with your junk! Gone on and sneak outta' here if you wanna'. I done took my hands off you and done left you n' the hands o' The Lord!"

And with that said, she took my kids and left. As soon as she pulled out of the driveway, I took off in search of a hit.

My Mama is praying woman. She believes what God says and there's no changing her mind once she's set on His Word. When she says she's leaving you in the hands of The Lord, all of her kids know that that means we're in trouble.

During my sober days, I kept my house spotless. The minute I took a hit, I began to turn my house into a pigsty. I would ramble through all the drawers in the house, pulling things out for no reason at all, leaving things in the middle of the floor. I would light cigarettes and leave them burning in every ashtray in the house. I'd cut out all the lights and go into a panic after each puff I took off the pipe. I was insane.

After smoking in my living room for two hours, I thought I heard a noise. I kept peeking through the windows, afraid that someone would knock on the door and interrupt my high. So, I gathered al my junk and went into the basement. There, still paranoid, I smoked for hours. All of a sudden I heard a voice ask me kindly and tenderly, **"Aren't you tired yet, Baby?"**

This wasn't a usual voice – it wasn't one of the demons I usually heard. I knew that because they were never concerned about my well-being. This was an audible voice, as if someone were sitting right next to me. I totally lost it! I thought my mother's premonition had come to pass – I thought I had really gone crazy.

I knew from that moment on that I would never, ever smoke crack cocaine again. I gathered all the crack I had left, the cigarettes, matches, and the bottle of Jack Daniels that I'd been drinking, and flushed it all down the toilet.

That was February 18, 1995.

# PART FOUR: A NEW BIRTH

# CHAPTER ONE:
# HEARING GOD'S VOICE

*"Now Samuel did not yet know the Lord, neither was the word of the Lord yet revealed unto him. And the LORD called Samuel again the third time. And he arose and went to Eli, and said, Here am I; for thou didst call me. And Eli perceived that the LORD had called the child"*
*I Samuel 3:7-8*

My baby girl, Desiree Dominique, was born February 23rd, 1995. During the first five days between my last hit and her birth, I was in a state of silent shock. I knew that Somebody was in that basement with me just as sure as I knew my name. I didn't see anybody, but I knew Someone was there. I was scared – really, really scared! I didn't tell anybody because I knew no one would believe me, so I sat around the house in almost complete silence. I didn't have much to say to anybody. My children kept asking, "What's wrong, Mommy? Are you okay?" I'd assure them that I was fine. Desiree's father watched me as if I were on a suicide watch. He stayed very close to me, afraid that I might try and hurt myself and the baby. I was acting that strange. I did try to tell him what I experienced in the basement, but Something stopped me right in the middle of the sentence. My mouth was moving but no sound came out. To top it all off, I went into labor almost four weeks early.

I was really scared, now. I had smoked a lot of cocaine five days prior to my first contraction. There could be no way that this baby could be born without cocaine being in her system. For the first time in a long time, I cried. Out of the pit of my soul, I cried. The tears would not stop coming. Something was happening to me and I felt strangely aware that eyes were watching me. I didn't feel threatened as I would when the monsters were near, but I knew I was not alone. Someone or Something was watching me, following my every move. Strangely, I didn't hear any voices. I found myself straining to hear, to see if any voice would say something, but I heard absolutely nothing. When you've been use to hearing voices in your head for years and suddenly you realize that you don't hear them anymore, it's really weird. In a way, I felt kind of deaf.

My labor pains were extremely painful. Plus, I had developed a pinched nerve in my left leg sometime during my pregnancy which was just as painful as the contractions. Desiree's father left the room to get a nurse to give me something for the pain. Suddenly, I felt as if Someone was standing over my right shoulder. I turned around and saw no one, but I felt a Presence. That's when I began to pray.

"God, please. I know I don't deserve it, but please have mercy on my baby. Please don't let any drugs be in her system, and I swear, God, I'll never do drugs again".

I got a response in the same Voice that I had heard in my basement:

*"That's what you said with you're your other two babies. I don't want you to just give up drugs. This time, I want you to surrender your life and your will to Me".*

Now, in all my years of going to church, I'd heard that God spoke to people, but never in a million years did I ever actually think that He would ever speak to me. Yet, I knew that I was hearing the Voice of God at that moment. Something was really happening to me that was harder for me to explain to myself than it would be for me to try and explain to somebody else. How could God actually be speaking to me? I thought to myself, "I really must be going crazy for real, now! God is holy, and there's no way He could want something like me!" So, I tried to pretend that nothing happened, but it was too late. God was ready to do a new thing in me.

Desiree's birth was the most painful of all the children I gave birth to. She came into the world fighting! Her father, my sister, and Ressie were all in the delivery room with me. The nurse kept telling me to stop pushing, but I told her I wasn't pushing. She kept insisting that I was, so finally I pushed myself up so I could see what was going on. As I looked down, I saw this little white hand beside Desiree's head – she was prying herself out of me! I was horrified and in shock as her head popped out and rolled around to look up at me. I was not pushing; she just seemed to ooze herself out! I began to scream at this point; "Oh my God! I'm having Rosemary's baby!!!" Once she was fully out, her arms and legs were flying all over the place as if she were a bit annoyed that someone was touching her. My older children were dark like me, but this little girl was so light I couldn't believe that I had her. She was cute, cuddly, and chubby, and I vowed that she would never see me on drugs.

During the next few days, I came to the realization that I was supposed to be doing something with my life other than throwing it away on drugs. I couldn't wait to get home to my kids. I began to see myself for who and what I really was at that time – a "crack head" who didn't appreciate all that God had done for me. I started remembering all the times that I had abandoned and neglected my children just so I could get high.

I saw myself stealing from my Mama's wallet. I had flashbacks to the times that I actually used crack in the basement of my church. I realized that I couldn't even remember how many men I'd slept with for drugs, not to mention their names. I felt so ashamed of myself. During the three days that I stayed in the hospital, I suffered from the horrible reality of what I had become and the devastating effects of what I had done to my family. I knew it was time to change, and I was completely ready.

# CHAPTER TWO: CRYING OUT TO GOD

*"In my distress I cried unto the LORD, and He heard me"*
*Psalms 120:1*

It was time to leave the hospital. The voices kept telling me, *"You'll never be free!! Stop playing! As soon as you get on the block, you'll go straight across the street and get a hit!"* I was so afraid that I didn't know what to do. I thought about signing myself into a rehabilitation center, but I knew I couldn't leave my kids with anybody that long. Somehow, I had to get myself together but I was deathly afraid that I would fail. My fear gave the devil ammunition to try and get me back in his grips once more. As soon as we got in the car, Dessy's father began accusing me of lying about him being her father. He declared that I didn't know who her father was and I was trying to trap him. Although I was with other men in the streets, I had sense enough to protect myself. Besides that fact, Desiree is the splitting image of her father.

The argument continued even after we got in the house. We had always argued before – he'd curse me out all the time, but I never paid him any attention. I just use to tune him out and go get high. The pressure to do so that day was extremely intense. I could taste cocaine in my mouth, and my stomach was getting all nervous, but I fought it. I began to curse back at him and all of a sudden, he hit me. Hard. I thought, "Oh no, not again! Not another man is ever gonna' hit me again and get away with it!" I ran into the bathroom, seriously considering how I was going to get him. There was a long slither of glass in the cabinet that had broken off of the mirror. I held it my hand as I was saying, "I'm gonna' kill him!" Suddenly, he pushed the bathroom door open and began daring me to cut him.

Something in me snapped. Normally, it would have been a fight, but this time was different. I couldn't even respond to him because I heard that now familiar basement Voice, saying, ***"This is what he wants. He wants a reason to kill you. Don't do it."*** He kept saying,*" **Don't do it, Child"**,* over and over again. Finally, I put the glass down, pushed past him and ran into my room, slamming the door. I fell on my knees and cried out unto God.

"Look, God! I feel real stupid talking and ain't nobody here in this room, but if You are Who my Mama's been saying You are, then You better show up and DO SOMETHING! I got $70 in my pocket and I wanna' get high! If You don't do somethin', when I come out of this room, one of us is going to jail and one of us is going to hell, cuz I wanna' kill this man! Now, I don't know You as The God Who can do the impossible, but I heard that You can do all things. I don't wanna' lose my kids! I really don't wanna' get high, I don't wanna' turn no more tricks, and I sure don't wanna' go to jail for killing nobody, but I ain't gonna' just let him hit me no more! Now, if You are Who You say You are, I need You to show up and help me out of this hell I'm in!"

It was maybe seven o'clock in the evening and it was dark outside. I never turned the light on in my room when I came in it, but suddenly, there was this radiant light that I not only saw but I also felt it. I may have stayed on that floor for about half an hour or so, but it felt like hours. Years of decay lifted from me as I began to feel a love and warmth that I'd never known before. My mind was like a movie that showed all these clips from the past – back to when I was seven – back to all the years of abuse – back to the lonely nights of crying – back to walking the streets. All the shame and all the years of pain just seemed to lift as if someone were pulling the covers off of my back. For the first time in my life, I knew beyond any shadow of a doubt that I was loved, that I was special, and that I was forgiven. I felt as if hundreds of thousands of people were all around me, smiling at me with hearts full of love. I felt the Presence of God and His angels around me, and I knew that I'd been changed. My boyfriend had been trying to open the door but it was supernaturally locked by God until He was done ministering to me.

It was supernatural because in the eight years that I lived at 914 Parkview Avenue, there were no locks on any of the bedroom doors.

# CHAPTER THREE: GETTING RID OF THE OLD

*"I beseech you therefore, brethren, by the mercies of God, that ye present your bodies a living sacrifice, holy, acceptable unto God, which is your reasonable service. And be not conformed to this world: but be ye transformed by the renewing of your mind, that ye may prove what is that good, and acceptable, and perfect, will of God"* ---Romans 12:1-2

To be able to share the past events with you is an honor and a privilege, and the One Who makes it possible is God. When I finally emerged from that bedroom, I was completely changed in one sense, but I had a lot of the old that had to die in order that Christ could live in me.

2Corintians 5:17 says, **"IF ANY MAN BE IN CHRIST, HE IS A NEW CREATURE: OLD THINGS HAVE PASSED AWAY; BEHOLD, ALL THINGS ARE BECOME NEW"**.

In that room on that floor, God gave me a new heart. I no longer wanted to be on drugs. I no longer wanted to throw my life away. I no longer wanted to abandon and neglect my kids. I no longer wanted to be a liar. I wanted to live. I wanted to be an honest, upright person, and I wanted to be a responsible parent. I told God that I didn't know how to be responsible, how to be a good mom, or how to stay off drugs, but I was willing to try anything as long as He would stay with me and be my Guide.

To say it was easy is an absolute lie. When I came out of that room, I couldn't walk. My body was completely worn out from years of abuse. I was physically exhausted, and I felt drained of every ounce of strength. I also could not talk without stammering. And oh, how I cried! I cried because I was changed and I knew it. I cried because I was ashamed. I cried because I realized I could finally feel something other than just the urge to get high. I cried because for the first time in my life I felt real love. I felt the close Presence of a God that loved me even though I had shunned Him for years. I cried because I was constantly hearing His reassuring Voice, speaking words of comfort and love. I cried because I was still alive, despite all the attempts I'd made to commit suicide – despite all the times people tried to kill me – despite the rotten way I had treated everyone one I knew, I was still alive, and God was saying that he loved me anyway! I had to find out more about this God.

I began to study the Bible and I knew God was with me because I really understood it. I knew a lot of Scripture because Mama always made sure we read the Bible as kids, and I use to like to boast about knowing the stories we'd talk about in Sunday School. But, I only knew the stories – I never knew The Man the stories talked about. I developed a new desire to study and to hear The Word. I stopped listening to the radio, and I stopped watching shows on T.V. that didn't teach me something about God. I began to renew my mind with The Word of God as Romans 12:2 teaches, and I no longer wanted to be around people who didn't want to talk about God.

In the midst of being "born again" (John 3:3), the devil was not willing to let me go. As I mentioned, I couldn't walk normally for about eight months. My boyfriend had to literally carry me to the bathroom. Although I was always hungry, I couldn't keep the food down properly for a month or two. I stayed out of church for a few weeks because I was embarrassed to go back. Everybody knew about me. I use to beg some of the members for money to get high, always lying when I said I'd pay them back. I was so thin, I looked anorexic. When I finally came to church, I heard people whisper as I walked by, but I was past caring about what people said. I wanted God and I wanted Him bad. I knew He loved me and I knew He'd fight my battles for me. 2Chronicles 20:15 says, **"BE NOT AFRAID NOR DISMAYED BY REASON OF THIS GREAT MULTITUDE; FOR THE BATTLE IS NOT YOURS, BUT GOD'S".** I knew that I was forgiven in God's eyes because 1John1:9 says, **"IF WE CONFESS OUR SINS, HE IS FAITHFUL AND JUST TO FORGIVE US OUR SINS,**

**AND TO CLEANSE US FROM ALL UNRIGHTEOUSNESS".** So, despite the nasty looks and the whispers, I went to every church service I could just to hear The Word of God. I was like a sponge – I soaked up The Word.

My daily thought life became a constant trial. I had to fight off the voices that suddenly reappeared, telling me I'd never make it and that I'd always be a crack head. Suddenly I had new enemies; my so-called friends and even some family members. I abused drugs for sixteen years. I had lied to my family time and time again saying I was done with drugs, only to relapse again. The people I associated with at that time never heard me talk about God before, so it was unbelievable to them that I had "found God" and was giving up "the life". Mama was reluctant to leave me alone with my own kids. She wasn't sure if I'd "fall off the wagon", as she use to say. My boyfriend had gone from Dr. Jekyll to Mr. Hyde. He constantly accused me of cheating on him with some guy. He became so paranoid about me being with other men that I couldn't go anywhere without him showing up. He'd ride up and down the block if I was at Mama's house, swearing he'd just seen some guy running out the back door of the house as he was pulling up. He would say I only wanted to go over my mother's so much because I was meeting up with my lover, accusing my family of covering up for me. It became unbearable for me and I was ready for him to move out of my house.

I tried to make it with him. I was grateful to him for all he'd done for me and my kids while I was using. He would always come to my rescue when I got into trouble in the streets, which was quite often back then. But suddenly, he had become a ranting maniac, going on and on about things that I just was not guilty of. It seemed the closer I got to God, the further apart we drifted from each other. I began trying to live like the Word says I should, and fornication is not the Will of God (see Galatians 5:19; I Corin-thians 6:13-18; I Thessalonians 4:3). Every time I opened The Bible, one of the Scriptures concerning fornication would pop up, and I soon realized that God was talking to me.

But, as I said; I was new in some areas, but a lot of my old ways kept popping up.

# CHAPTER FOUR: YIELD NOT TO TEMPTATION

*"What? Know ye not that your body is the temple of the Holy Ghost which is in you, which ye have of God, and ye are not your own? For ye are bought with a price: therefore glorify God in your body, and in your spirit, which are God's"*
*I Corinthians 6:19-20*

Although I'd been raised in church, I'd never known Jesus as my personal Savior. I didn't even know what that meant. I surely had no idea what it meant to be filled with The Holy Ghost, or to be baptized in The Spirit. I knew that people said that once you were baptized and you believed that Jesus rose from the dead, you were saved. I knew people said that you were suppose to "change from your wicked ways", but I didn't see any change in the people who claimed they were saved. Remember: I got drunk with church folks; I got high with church folks; I sold drugs to church folks; I had affairs with deacons and even pastors in the church. The pastor of the church I attended when I first came to Christ did preach the Gospel, but I knew that he was secretly having affairs and flirting with different women in the church. To say that I was a bit confused is an understatement. I was downright disillusioned, and the devil had a field day with me.

By the end of 1996, my boyfriend had moved out and my hormones were running all over the place. Abstaining from sexual intercourse was a very big challenge for me because I had grown accustomed to having a man in my bed. The old voices came back: *"What's wrong with you, girl?! You can't make it without a man! Sure, giving up drugs is okay, but let's not get crazy! You cannot go without sex! Surely God wants you to be happy! Go 'head, chile'! Call up one of your old friends! Just one night ain't gonna' hurt you none!"*

For a while, I resisted the devil, but I wasn't spiritually mature enough to know how clever and smooth the devil really is. 2 Corinthians 11: 14-15 says, **"AND NO MARVEL; FOR SATAN HIMSELF IS TRANSFORMED AS AN ANGEL OF LIGHT. THEREFORE, IT IS NO GREAT THING IF HIS MINISTERS ALSO BE TRANSFORMED AS MINISTERS OF DARKNESS".** I had read this Scripture but I didn't get it way down deep in my spirit. Because I was vulnerable, and I did not seek God's opinion, and I did what I wanted to do and not what God's Word said I should do, I became involved with a married man. You may be asking yourself why I would do something so out of the will of God when I was supposed to be trying to please Him. As I said; Satan, our enemy, is very clever, and he's a master at seduction.

This man befriended me, told me he saw God in me, and encouraged me with to continue to keep holding on to my sobriety. He spoke great swelling words of wisdom into my broken spirit. He made me feel pretty again. He complimented me on my appearance, and praised me for being such a good mother. Back then, I was still under the condemnation of the devil. I felt so horrible about the way I treated my kids during addiction, so for someone to say that I was now doing a good job as a mother made me feel like a million dollars. My self-esteem was so low that depression was a constant companion. To receive a compliment of any kind gave me a false sense of worth. I hadn't fully realized that my worth and identity are in Christ and not man. So, once again, I fell for the flattery of a lying tongue.

This man and I began a torrid affair which lasted only a few months. He was insatiable and so was I. We cared for each other tremendously, or so we thought. Because of God's purpose for my life, He intervened and rescued me once again. All of a sudden, "Pastor" avoided me. He stopped calling and he wouldn't take any of my phone calls. So, I'd go to his office at the church where he pastured, only to be told by his secretary that he wasn't receiving any visitors. After a few weeks of rejection, I finally gave up.

I was devastated. Once again, I felt used and discarded like an old newspaper. The old voices were getting louder and louder, telling me that it was no use – I'd never be anything other than a worthless whore. I felt too ashamed to pray and the desire to give up was very strong. I thought that once I stopped using drugs, everything would be alright. I had experienced an encounter with God, so I thought that was all I needed in order to live free of the voices, the guilt, and the shame of my past. Yet, here I was, creating new guilt and shame for myself and I wasn't even using anymore. What was I to do now? I was drug free, but I was still so low down that I'd had an affair with a married man – and a pastor at that! I began to feel that I was a hopeless case. Once again, depression was right there to befriend me. Finally, I began to call on the Name of Jesus, and he rescued me once again. He gave me the strength to keep pressing toward the mark for the prize of the high calling of God which is in Christ Jesus (Philippians 4:19).

I went back to my old church where Mama and Ressie were still attending. Since I was not fully submitted to God or His Word, I was still an easy prey for the devil and vulnerable to his schemes. I truly wanted to do right by my kids, to be a good mother, and for them to have a dad. So, I kept seeking for a husband, and I thought I had found one.

This man was not my husband and I knew it, but I was tired of being alone. He was seeing someone but they weren't serious, so we began dating. We were an item for over a year, and all of a sudden, he married someone else. Out of no where. No excuses. No explanation. I went to South Carolina for my uncle's funeral, and when I came back, I found out that he had proposed to the girl that he said he wasn't serious about. It was the straw that broke the camel's back.

God had my attention. I would not sleep with another man until God I got married. That was in 1998.

# CHAPTER FIVE: ISSUES

*"No man putteth new wine into old bottles: else the new wine doth burst the bottles, and the wine is spilled, and the bottles will be marred: but new wine must be put into new bottles"*
*Mark 2:22*

Many people do not realize that those who come out of addiction have serious issues. How do you live day by day without the escape from reality that the drug provided? How do you socialize with people that have never used drugs? How do you get rid of the shame and guilt? How do you hold your head up in public? These are the questions that constantly consume the thoughts of people coming out of addiction.

Addiction is considered as a sickness or a disease, as Narcotics and Alcohol Anonymous suggests. Whereas medical science views the cause of sickness and disease to be physiological or psychosomatic, the Bible reveals that some illnesses are spiritually related. There is a two-fold problem. One is sin, which affects our spiritual and physical make-up (John 5: 5-14). The other is Satan, the adversary of God and the believers of God (Acts 10: 38; Mark 9: 17, 20, 25: Luke 13: 11-12; Acts 19: 11-12).

Acts 10: 38 says Jesus healed those oppressed of the devil, and I fully believe that a crack addict fits that description. The devil has a host of demons that aid him in holding people captive. We are not fighting with flesh and blood when dealing with addiction, but against unseen wicked forces that delight in keeping people in bondage (Ephesians 6: 12). In order to help people get delivered and stay delivered, we must realize that there is more to it than just casting out the demons of drugs and alcohol.

During the beginning chapters of this book, I showed you a pattern. I did not just up and decide to use drugs one day. From a little child, I was influenced by the presence of demons into an ungodly lifestyle. Unless the people of God are taught how to identify and correctly discern the presence and the work of the demonic forces that operate against us, the addict will suffer in the hands of the devil indefinitely. I sought the help of many pastors of various churches for deliverance. Many hands were laid on me in Jesus' Name in an attempt to cast out the demon of addiction, but I'd relapse time and time again. When God secluded me in my house on Parkview Avenue – after He had shut me off from all outside influences – after he had allowed my friends and family to forsake me – after I had exhausted every avenue of help, aid, and assistance without any consistent results, and after much prayer and fasting, He began revealing to me a way of life that has kept me saved and sober for over sixteen years.

Mark 9: 17-29 reveals the story of a man that brought his son to the disciples of Jesus to be delivered from an evil spirit. The disciples were anointed men with authority to cast out devils (Mark 3: 13-15), yet they failed, on this occasion, to relieve this young boy of demonic oppression. Why? In verse 29, Jesus says, **"THIS KIND CAN COME FORTH BY NOTHING BUT PRAYER AND FASTING"**.

There must be a consistent, continuous lifestyle of prayer and fasting unto God in order to develop a keen sense of discernment. Webster's dictionary describes "discern" as "the ability to see or notice something that is not clear; to be able to understand something that is not immediately obvious".

The Spirit of God enables us to properly discern things that are not readily obvious to us and others, but we must completely empty ourselves of ourselves in order to be filled with God's Holy Spirit. It wasn't until I became filled with the Holy Spirit that I discerned that addiction was only an outward manifestation of the bitterness, rejection, and hatred that I'd held inside my heart from a child. People don't just turn to drugs and stay on drugs without a cause. There has to be a seed that was planted somewhere at some point in a person's life that took root and began to grow (See Matthew chapter 13). Drugs provide a temporary escape from the reality of life's circumstances. Alcohol numbs the senses so that our emotions are unaware of the pain of abuse. When we are detached from reality, and numb to our emotions, it is difficult to get in touch with what's really going on in our hearts.

Romans 12: 1-2 says, **"I BESEECH YOU THEREFORE, BRETHERN, BY THE MERCIES OF GOD, THAT YE PRESENT YOUR BODIES A LIVING SACRIFICE, HOLY AND ACCEPTABLE UNTO GOD, WHICH IS YOUR REASONABLE SERVICE. AND BE NOT CONFORMED TO THIS WORLD, BUT BE YE TRANSFORMED BY THE RENEWING OF YOUR MIND, THAT YE MAY PROVE WHAT IS THAT GOOD AND ACCEPTABLE AND PERFECT WILL OF GOD".** I had come to realize that if I was going to live a new life in Christ, then I had to separate myself from anyone who did not want to sell out to God.

Deuteronomy 28: 1-9 says, *"AND IT SHALL COME TO PASS, IF THOU HEARKEN DILIGENTLY TO THE VOICE OF THE LORD THY GOD, TO OBSERVE TO DO ALL HIS COMMANDMENTS… THAT THE LORD THY GOD WILL SET THEE ON HIGH ABOVE ALL NATIONS OF THE EARTH; AND <u>ALL THESE BLESSINGS SHALL COME ON THEE AND OVERTAKE THEE</u>, IF THOU SHALT HEARKEN UNTO THE VOICE OF THE LORD THY GOD. BLESSED SHALT THOU BE IN THE CITY, AND <u>BLESSED</u> SHALT THOU BE IN THE FIELD. BLESSED SHALL BE THE FRUIT OF THY BODY… THY GROUND…THY CATTLE, AND THE INCREASE OF THY KINE, AND THE FLOCKS OF THY SHEEP. <u>BLESSED</u> SHALL BE THY BASKET AND THY STORE. <u>BLESSED</u> SHALT THOU BE WHEN THOU COMEST IN AND <u>BLESSED</u> SHALT THOU BE WHEN THOU GOEST OUT. THE LORD SHALL CAUSE THINE ENEMIES THAT RISE UP AGAINST THEE TO BE SMITTEN BEFORE THY FACE; THEY SHALL COME OUT AGAINST THEE ONE WAY, AND SHALL FLEE BEFORE THEE SEVEN WAYS. <u>THE LORD SHALL COMMAND THE BLESSING UPON THEE</u>…IN ALL THAT THOU SETTEST THINE HAND UNTO…THE LORD SHALL ESTABLISH THEE A HOLY PEOPLE…IF THOU SHALT KEEP THE COMMANDMENTS OF THE LORD THY GOD, AND WALK IN ALL HIS WAYS".*

I started to believe that life could really be worth living if I just obeyed God and put my trust in Him. As I yielded myself to Him, He began to show me His power. Colossians 3:1-10 taught me to set my affections on things above, where Christ sits on the right hand of God. I began to forget about my past and I became eager to know more about God. My life is now hid with Christ in God (Colossians 3:3), and I am dead to sin (Romans 6:1-4). My mind was becoming transformed by the Word of God, and I no longer wanted to live to please "me, myself, and I". I wanted to live a life that is pleasing to God. After all I had done to shun Him, He still loved me and He kept me. He wasn't ashamed to call me His own, and I am no longer ashamed to be called "HIS".

Colossians 3:5-8 teaches, "**MORTIFY THEREFORE YOUR MEMBERS ON THE EARTH: FORNICATION, UNCLEANNESS, INORDINATE AFFECTION, EVIL CONCUPISCENCE, AND COVETEOUSNESS WHICH IS IDOLATRY…PUT OFF ALL THESE; ANGER, WRATH, MALICE, BLASPHEMY, FILTHY COMMUNICATION OUT OF YOUR MOUTH"**.

I began to be continually aware of my actions. I didn't want to go back to my old way of living, so I sought the help of the Lord day by day, moment by moment. I asked the Holy Spirit's opinion about everything: where to eat, and what to eat; what to wear, and what not to wear; who to talk to, who not to talk to, and what to say to the people He led me to talk to. I didn't just "play saved" anymore. I was saved for real, and I determined to live out the rest of my days on this earth to the glory of God.

# PART FIVE: FROM THEN UNTIL NOW

# CHAPTER ONE: LIVING BY HIS PRECEPTS

*"When wisdom entereth into thine heart, and knowledge is pleasant unto thy soul; Discretion shall preserve thee, understanding shall keep thee"*
*Proverbs 2:10-11*

I have made a lot of mistakes. Big ones. I still do. But God's mercy has kept me from going back to the things of the world. Jesus told His disciple, Peter, in Luke 22: 31-32 that Satan desired to have him in order to sift him as wheat, in an attempt to destroy the ministry that God was preparing him for. Jesus prayed for Peter and told him, **"WHEN THOU ART CONVERTED, STRENGHTHEN THY BRETHREN"**.

I believe that the events of my past were allowed by God to take place in order that He may be glorified for delivering me out of Satan's clutches. I believe that the reason I failed to kill myself was because Jesus is at the right hand of the Father making intercession (praying) for me (Romans 8:34). I know that a part of the purpose He has ordained for my life is to strengthen my brothers and sisters, to encourage people not to lose heart or give up. No matter what you've been involved in, or how far down in the mud you've gone, Jesus is able to pick you up, dust you off, and cause you to live a victorious life. Despite what the devil meant for my bad, God has always turned it all around to cause it to work out for my good.

Although I was living my life for Jesus, life did not turn into a bed of roses. It's funny how sometimes we are led to believe that once you come to Christ your life will become peaches and cream. I believe a lot of

Christians fail to live the abundant life because we are disillusioned about the Christian life in general. Jesus told us in John 16:33 that we would have tribulation in this world, but we can be of good cheer because He has overcome the world. The apostle Paul tells us in Galatians 5:16 to **"WALK IN THE SPIRIT, AND YE SHALL NOT FULFILL THE LUSTS OF THE FLESH"**. This is easier said than done.

It is still a challenge for me at times to allow the Spirit of God to have complete control over my daily life. We are all good at putting on appearances and wearing masks around those people that we hold dear to us. Some of us don't like to let people see us as we really are. If we are going through a personal trial in our home, such as problems with our children or in our marriages, we lie and tell people that everything is alright. The reality is that sometimes, life can be hard, especially when you try with everything in you to do the will of God and you keep getting hit with blow after blow of disappointment. Family members can hurt us badly by the wrong choices they make. Through the years I have been mistreated by people I thought were friends. Before I came to Christ, I expected to be mistreated by people in the world because I knew that it was every man for himself. What was a shock for me was to be used and abused by people who called themselves saints. God has had to deal with me mightily concerning this because I was ready to leave the church countless times on account of being mistreated by people.

Jesus said in Matthew 10: 24-25, **"THE DISCIPLE IS NOT ABOVE HIS MASTER, NOR THE SERVANT ABOVE HIS LORD. IT IS ENOUGH FOR THE DISCIPLE THAT HE BE AS HIS MASTER, AND THE SERVANT AS HIS LORD. IF THEY HAVE CALLED THE MASTER OF THE HOUSE BEELZEBUB, HOW MUCH MORE SHALL THEY CALL THEM OF HIS HOUSEHOLD?"**

This scripture informs us that Jesus was called Beelzebub, which means the prince of devils, by the people of the church. It was the scribes, the Pharisees, and the elders of the church that persecuted Jesus and condemned Him to death on the cross. He was rejected by the very people He came to give His life for. If the Son of God was mistreated, we must be prepared to go through the same trials as He did. But we don't have to lose heart because if He is with us, we can do all things through Him (Philippians 4:19).

Towards the end of 1998, I went back to the church where Mama and Ressie attended. Yes, the very church in which just a few short years before I was the laughingstock. It was here that God called me to preach the gospel. I hadn't really accepted the call; I ran for a while. I couldn't believe that God wanted to use me. I had such an awful past I thought He couldn't possibly use me. There is something about God's glory on your life; other people see it before you do. The members of my church began telling me that God was going to use me to preach and tell people what He'd done in my life. The pastor I was under did not believe in women preachers, and he made sure I knew it. Every Sunday morning, no matter what his text was, he somehow ended up during his message saying, "Cheryl, don't let nobody tell you that you've been called to preach just because you can sing and play! You stay right there on that piano, girl! God can use you right where you are!" It got to the point that I became so infuriated by it that I approached him in love about it. He did not respond in love. He became so angry that I was shocked. I was hurt and very angry I couldn't believe that a pastor could be so evil. I also began to seriously take a look at his walk with the Lord. Matthew 7:20 says, **"BY THEIR FRUITS YE SHALL KNOW THEM"**. This man had more than a few rotten apples on his tree. I decided it was time to go to another church, and I began to seek the Lord about it.

# CHAPTER TWO: NEW DIRECTIONS

*"For My thoughts are not your thoughts, neither are your ways My ways, saith the Lord"*
*-Isaiah 55:8*

During the next few months, God led me to church after church. I realize why now, but at the time, I had no clue what God was doing. All I knew is that when He said go, I went. My family thought I was absolutely crazy, and I remember often asking God was I. I mean, I was the only person I knew that was being led by God to a different church Sunday after Sunday. Finally, God showed me why.

There are a great many buildings that are called churches, but the Presence and the Power of God are not there. God was preparing me to teach people how to seek and follow His Presence and His Power, and not what "looked like church". With my background, I could spot a phony usually on sight. The life I use to live taught me how to pick up what I call "sha-nana banigans" – that's just a word I picked up from my niece, which simply means "foolishness". I believe part of the reason why people fail in living a victorious life in Christ is because we follow the traditions of men. We can know something is wrong, yet because we are comfortable, we refuse to address it, in fear that we might hurt someone's feelings.

I was not willing to settle for just a "form of godliness" (2Timothy 3:1-5). I wanted the real Presence, the real Power of God. I wanted what the Word of God says I can have, and I refuse to settle for less. When I started talking like that, I upset some people. Most of the churches I went to in those days were full of people who were content with just "going to church on Sunday". They didn't really believe in miracles, or the laying on of hands, and especially women being used by God. I don't know what Bible they were reading, but I was glad that I wasn't reading it. I had a hunger in me for more, and God satisfied my appetite.

I joined a church where the Word of God was taught with power. Signs and wonders were a regular occurrence, and I was happy for a while. But I kept sensing that there was more. I wanted to belong to a church that was not only concerned about the members, but had a concern for the lost. I felt a burden for people who were still strung out, still hopeless, still stuck with no one to help them get out. It was during this time that God began to show me visions where I was preaching to people all over the world. I saw myself before so many people, teaching the Word of God. I saw myself ministering to hurting, broken women. I began going to nursing homes and to the prisons, sharing the gospel of Jesus Christ with people who seemed so glad that somebody took the time out to encourage them. I felt like I was being born again all over again. Then, a funny thing happened – God said I had to go back to my old church.

I was thrown completely into a whirlwind! I thought, "God, surely, You can't really be serious! I mean, after all that I'd gone through there, why would You send me back?" It was the first of many hard things that the Lord has asked me to do.

Oh! Didn't you know that God asks us to do some hard things? Let's look at Abraham. **"AND HE SAID, TAKE NOW THY SON, THINE ONLY SON ISAAC, WHOM THOU LOVEST, AND GET THEE TO THE LAND OF MORIAH; AND OFFER HIM THERE FOR A BURNT OFFERING UPON ONE OF THE MOUNTAINS WHICH I WILL TELL THEE OF"** (Genesis 22:2).

God had promised Abraham that through his seed, Isaac, all the nations of the earth would be blessed, yet He turned around and told Abraham to take Isaac and offer him up to Him as a sacrifice. If you read the entire story, you'll find out that just as Abraham was about to kill his son, God showed him a ram in the bush which he used as the sacrifice. God wanted to see if Abraham loved him enough to give up his dearly beloved son (Genesis 22:3-14). Abraham passed the test.

That might seem like a stretch to you because God just asked me to give up my pride and go back and fellowship with people who hurt me. But I want you to know that to humble ourselves and be obedient to a leader can be just as painful as it was for Abraham to offer up his son. The flesh does not want to humble itself. Ever. It will fight you tooth and nail. The only way to overcome it is to deny how you feel, what you think, and what you want to do and trust God.

Jesus says in Luke 9:23, "**IF ANY MAN WILL COME AFTER ME, LET HIM DENY HIMSELF, TAKE UP HIS CROSS DAILY, AND FOLLOW ME**".

That's what God was asking me to do. I had to trust Him enough to know that He is God and He loves me. If He wanted me to go back and humble myself under a leader whose heart I'm sure He knows better than I do, He must plan on teaching me something that I needed to know. I had to remember Romans 8:28: **"AND WE KNOW THAT ALL THINGS WORK TOGETHER FOR GOOD TO THEM THAT LOVE GOD, TO THEM WHO ARE THE CALLED ACCORDING TO HIS PURPOSE"**.

I had been asking God to make me like Him. Boy, oh boy! God gave me what I asked for! Jesus died for the ungodly. He died for the sinners. He died for the unlovable. He gave me the opportunity to learn how to love the unlovable. He loved me when I was unlovable. He showed me how to love my enemies, to pray for those who hated me and despitefully used me (Matthew 5:44). I learned what it really means to be like Jesus.

And then, in 2002, He said it was time to leave Ohio.

# CHAPTER THREE: WHERE HE LEADS ME I WILL FOLLOW

*"And Peter answered Him and said, 'Lord, if it be Thou, bid me to come unto Thee on the water'. And He(Jesus) said 'Come'. And when Peter was come down out of the ship, he walked on the water, to go to Jesus"-Matthew 14:28-29*

I began working at a daycare center in 1997. God had impressed upon me some years earlier that children were my passion. I love children, and they love me. Everywhere I go, kids are drawn to me. One day at work, I began having headaches. They had gotten so bad that I went to the doctor and underwent a series of testing which revealed that there was absolutely nothing wrong with me. They found no reason why my head hurt so badly that I could barely open my eyes. This was two weeks after God told me to leave. With me being so spiritual, I just knew that God couldn't be telling me to leave Ohio! He knew all the work I was doing in that town! Not only was I being used to bring people to Christ, I was on a good job where everybody loved me. I was instrumental in the turn-around of many wayward children in the daycare center where I worked so faithfully. Besides that, I had just moved into a brand new house. I had just gotten it to look like I wanted it to look with beautiful furniture in every room and plush carpet on all the floors. Surely God couldn't be telling me to give all that up! Surely it had to be the devil! He was just jealous that God was blessing me. Well, I tell you what! I made up my mind that I wasn't going anywhere! After all, who was going to take care of my mother? Who was going to look after Ressie? No, I couldn't go off and leave them all by themselves! I had to be there and make sure everything went the way it was supposed to go.

There is one thing that God will not tolerate. He will not share His glory with anybody else. As long as we try to be God, He cannot be. The first commandment tells us that we are to have no other God but Him (Exodus 20). Whenever we put our own ideas and opinions over what He tells us to do, we make ourselves out to be gods. I had to learn the hard way that when God says He is going to use you, He means exactly what He says. It would be better for us if we just yield to His way and let Him decide what's best for us. When all is said and done, we will see that His way is the best way.

I finally got the idea that maybe it was God Who was trying to get me to move to another place. After all, He was the One Who showed me in the dreams how I'd be traveling. I just realized that I couldn't win a fight with the Creator of the universe, so I said yes to Him. I had a little talk with Jesus.

I went in to my employers office and told him that it was my last day. I told him that I felt God was calling me to take on a new venture. By this time, my co-workers had come to know and believe that God was with me and that I had a real relationship with Him. With sadness I said my good-byes.

I went home and laid on my sofa, and said, "God, if this is You, tell me where You want me to go and I'll go". At that very moment, the telephone rang. It was a girl I grew up in church with in New York. She said she had been trying to get in touch with me for over a year, and that God had put me in her spirit. She began telling me everything that I'd been through in the last three years, beginning with what I was going through in my body. She said that God told her to tell me that He was going to use me to speak to broken and hurting women, that I was going to have to travel many different places and tell others what He had done in my life. She asked me to come and visit her in Delaware, just to see if I liked it. She didn't invite me to stay, but just come for a visit. She said, "Who knows! Maybe you won't want to go back!" I completely lost it. I knew it was God.

My Nadia had lost her hearing in her right ear, and was slowly losing hearing in the left one. She was attending a school in Youngstown that didn't specialize in working with deaf and hard of hearing children. I told the woman about this and she said she was sure that Delaware had a facility that could accommodate Nadia's needs. She said she'd find out and call me back. When I hung up the phone, I was in a semi-shock state. I knew it was God, but I still had to be sure. I told Him, "God, if this is You, when she calls back tomorrow, let her have not only the name of the school, but the number to the school so I can talk to the people myself".

Sure enough, when she called the next day, she not only had the name and number of Delaware's School for the Deaf, but she had the school's guidance counselor on three-way to talk to me! When we got off the phone, I was so excited I almost threw the phone across the room. I jumped and danced and cried all at the same time. I knew for sure without any question that I was actually hearing from God, that He was actually talking to me, and that He was getting me ready for the experience of a lifetime!

I was getting ready to move to a city that I didn't even know where in the world it was on the map! But how was I going to leave my entire family and go someplace where I knew absolutely no one?

Then, I heard what had become my dearest comfort – that now familiar basement Voice, saying, **"TRUST ME, CHILD"**.

I was slowly but surely coming to really trust and rely on that Voice.

The next morning, I made reservations to go to Delaware by bus.

# CHAPTER FOUR: NEW HORIZONS

*"I will bring the blind by the way that they knew not; I will lead them in paths that they have not known: I will make darkness light before them, and crooked things straight. These things will I do unto them, and not forsake them"*
*Isaiah 42:16*

I sat my children down and discussed with them what the Lord was dealing with me about. I told them that I believed that He had more for us than what we were limited to in Youngstown. The schools there were horrible, the jobs were scarce, and the average salary was way below what I desired. I told them that we were going to Delaware just to see if things looked better there. They quickly asked if we were coming back. They were concerned about leaving their Granny, Ressie, and all of their cousins. I told them we'd see what the Lord had in store for us.

Telling my Mama and Ressie was the hardest thing I ever had to do. They both knew without me saying that I might not be coming back. It's hard trying to put in words the weirdness I felt. I love my family tremendously. They were all I had. They were my comfort zone. Ressie and I were not only like sisters; we were best friends. I could always count on her to be there when I couldn't find anybody else. Good, bad, or indifferent, it was me and Ressie against the world. Mama is like a blanket that keeps me warm on a cold winter's night. She always has a word in due season to inspire me to keep on pressing on. When I told her that I was considering relocating, she just looked at me for a moment. Then, she said,

"Cherie, go where God leads you. I'm gonna' miss you, but I gotta' trust God that He'll take care of you all".

On Friday, July 6, 2002, my children and I boarded the bus for Wilmington, Delaware. We arrived the next day and we were very excited. The friends we were staying with met us at the bus station and we went to their home. It was much different than what I had expected. They lived in a town house, which connected to other homes. The kids thought it was strange, too. They'd never been in an apartment complex like that. The houses in Ohio were separated. Our first night there, we talked about the church that they attended. I didn't know that my friends had told their church families all about me. They said everyone was anxious to meet me, to hear me sing and play the piano. I was a bit taken uneasy by that. I had no interest in becoming affiliated with any churches too quickly. I had made up my mind that I would not ever join another church if the pastor was not fully sold out to God. I refuse to be under phony, wishy-washy leadership. I was assured that I would enjoy the services and the people. My girlfriend attended one church and her husband attended another. Naturally, she assumed that I was going to go to her church, and so did I. But, on that first evening, God spoke to me as I was studying my scriptures and said that I had to go to service with my girlfriend's husband. With no questions asked, I obeyed and went to Higher Ground Holy Christian Church, under the leadership of Pastor Linda Henry.

I will never forget that day. The kids were excited because there weren't many women preachers in Youngstown, and I couldn't think of one woman pastor there. Sunday School was very refreshing because the lesson was taught with power. The kids were very attentive as if they were enjoying it. The praise and worship service was phenomenal! We were thoroughly enjoying the service. Suddenly, I felt a rushing of wind to my left. I turned around towards the direction where I felt the breeze coming from to see this woman coming out of the office with two or three other women behind her. I actually saw the Power and the Presence of God following her. She had this glow that made her radiate. Immediately, God began speaking to me. He said, *"**This is the woman that I'm going to use to propel you into your destiny**"*. God has given me the gift of discernment, the ability to see what is not readily visible, the ability to see and discern the difference between the Presence of God and Satan. This woman was clearly a mighty woman of God. During the remainder of the service, I was actually holding a private conversation with God as I watched this woman flow under His Power. The sermon she presented was brought forth intelligently, with accuracy and power. God used her to speak prophetically into many people's lives that morning. She called people up and began to tell them what the Lord was sharing with her concerning their lives and the people responded with shouts of praise. During the entire time, God and I were still in private conversation. He kept telling me that this is where He wanted me to be. He said this woman would be a mother to me and nurture me in the spirit. He said she would introduce me to things in the spirit that He had been showing me for years.

All I could do was stare in amazement. I kept saying, "God, You can't possibly expect me to walk with this woman! Do You SEE the anointing that's on her life? How am I to travel with this lady, God?! I don't even know her, and she doesn't know me! Her ministers don't look like they'd welcome me to the fold, either, God! That one lady looks like her watch dog! You gotta' be kidding, God! I must be tripping! Okay, God. If this is You, let her call me up there and let her tell me what You're telling me".

Just as she was giving the benediction, she called me up front and confirmed not only what God was saying to me during the service; she went back to my childhood – to the bathroom thing. She even described the pain I felt having to hide it for so long. She told me that my family had taken me as far as they could take me. She said God had greater work for me to do and that He would send me to many nations, spreading the gospel. When she told me not to worry about my mother and my niece and that I could trust God to keep His promise to take care of them, I fell out flat on the floor and worshipped.

My life has never been the same since that day, July 7, 2002.

# CHAPTER FIVE: A BRAND NEW LIFE

*"Remember not the former things, neither consider the things of old. Behold, I will do a new thing; now it shall spring forth; shall ye not know it? I will even make a way in the wilderness, and rivers in the desert"-Isaiah 43:18-19*

It is now nine years later. Through Higher Ground Ministries, International, under the leadership of Apostle Linda Henry and the late Bishop Nathaniel Henry, I am now an Elder of the church, with a Bachelor's degree in Theology from Higher Ground Bible Institute, and married to their son, Deacon David A. Brown, Sr. We were married July 10, 2004 and I am now the mother of six. God has blessed me with three other children who I consider my own – JeNae Dashawn, David Jr., and LaMeka Andrea. I am also the very proud "Mom-Mom" of Terry White III, TraNae LeAsia White, and Isaivian Jamal Thomas. I am one of the Youth Advisors of our church and the Minister of Music. After working as a Toddler Teacher at One Step Ahead Daycare Center for three years, I now own my own home daycare center. God gave me the vision of Chosen Gener8tion Childcare Facility, and soon I will begin looking for a building to expand and fulfill the vision. With my Apostle, I have traveled to Florida, Oklahoma, Connecticut, California, where I met Prophetess Juanita Bynum, West Virginia, Washington, D.C., Pennsylvania, Georgia, New Jersey, Alabama, and many cities in Maryland. We've recorded a gospel CD/DVD with gospel recording artist Dorothy Norwood in June, 2010. God uses me to preach the Word to broken, hurting men and women. I have had many people come to me and thank me for sharing what God has done in my life with them. I am no longer an huge embarrassment to my family, and I am no longer ashamed of myself.

Me – the ex-crack head, now a licensed minister of the Gospel. Me – the former prostitute, now witnessing to prostitutes, telling them they don't have to stay in the shape they're in. Me - the girl who had lesbian affairs, now reaching out to those who thought homosexuality and lesbianism would forever be their life, leading them into the arms of Jesus. Me – the girl who had low self-esteem, now confident of this one thing: "**HE THAT HAS BEGUN A GOOD WORK IN ME WILL PERFORM IT UNTIL THE DAY OF JESUS CHRIST**" (Philippians 1:6).

I titled this book "The Re-making of An Addict" because that is exactly what God has done. He made me over again. I am a **"NEW CREATURE IN CHRIST: OLD THINGS HAVE PASSED AWAY; BEHOLD, ALL THINGS (HAVE) BECOME NEW"** (2Corintians 5:17).

Jeremiah 33:3 says, **"CALL UNTO ME, AND I WILL ANSWER THEE, AND SHOW THEE GREAT AND MIGHTY THINGS, WHICH THOU KNOWEST NOT"**.

Dear reader, no matter what you've done or how long you've done it, God can rescue you not only from Satan, but also from yourself. I was my biggest enemy. **<u>Although many events led to me winding up in my former lifestyle, the choice to stay so long was nobody's fault but mine. We may originally start out as a victim, but some of us remain victims by choice.</u>** We don't believe that we deserve anything better than what has been dished out to us. When offered a life jacket, some of us prefer to sink instead of swim. For a long time, I chose to believe all the lies that the devil had told me. I tried many self-help groups, Narcotics Anonymous, even acupuncture, and none of it helped me. After coming to the end of myself, I made a conscious decision to accept Jesus Christ as my Lord and Savior. He has never failed me. He has kept every promise that He made me.

Please do not misunderstand me. There are still some things I'm waiting on, but I have no doubt that He will bring it all to pass. Life has not been a flowery bed of roses. I've had my share of ups and downs, and I still have some issues that I need God's help to work through. But, with Jesus, I know I am not alone. He walks with me and talks with me and tells me that I am His very own. As I mentioned earlier, Jesus never said we'd never have problems, but He has promised to be with us through our problems. He will see you through every storm that comes your way, and He will lead you safely to a peaceful shore, if you would just **TRUST HIM**.

Maybe you've been hurt more seriously than I have. Maybe you've suffered grievously at the hands of a cruel parent or spouse. Maybe you've been abused by a family member or someone close to you, or maybe you've lost a parent, a child, or a loved one, and you feel that you should just end it all. To you I say, **TRY JESUS**.

Romans 10: 8-10 says, **"THE WORD IS NIGH (NEAR) THEE, EVEN IN THY MOUTH, AND IN THY HEART; THAT IS THE WORD WE PREACH; THAT IF THOU SHALT CONFESS WITH THY MOUTH THE LORD JESUS, AND SHALT BELIEVE IN THINE HEART THAT GOD HATH RAISED HIM FROM THE DEAD, THOU SHALT BE SAVED. FOR <u>WITH THE HEART</u> MAN BELIEVETH UNTO RIGHTEOUSNESS; AND <u>WITH THE MOUTH</u> CONFESSION IS MADE UNTO SALVATION"**.

In John 14:14, Jesus says, <u>**"IF THOU ASK ANYTHING IN MY NAME, I WILL DO IT"**</u>.

All God asks of you is to **BELIEVE THAT HE IS ABLE TO DO ALL THINGS.** If you don't know Jesus Christ as your personal Lord and Savior, and you are ready to stop trying to do things your way and ready to let Him have control of your life, repeat this prayer with me:

"**LORD JESUS, I CONFESS THAT I AM A SINNER AND I NEED TO BE SAVED. I HAVE TRIED MY OWN WAY FOR YEARS AND IT JUST DOESN'T WORK. I BELIEVE THAT YOU DIED ON THE CROSS FOR MY SINS AND THAT YOU ROSE FROM THE GRAVE WITH ALL POWER TO FORGIVE ME OF MY SINS AND TO CLEAN ME FROM ALL UNRIGHTEOUSNESS. I NOW INVITE YOU TO COME INTO MY HEART AND TAKE UP RESIDENCE. I SURRENDER MY HEART AND MY WILL TO YOU AND I AM NOW READY TO BEGIN LIVING LIFE AS YOU SEE FIT**".

<u>**Welcome to the family of the Body of Christ**</u>! I pray that you will now walk in the newness of life and begin living the abundant life that God has promised to us(John 10:10). Pray and ask God to lead you to a Bible believing church, where you can learn His Word and grow in the knowledge of His Will.

To those readers who are already in the family, **BE ENCOURAGED!** You can make it through anything with Jesus in your life. Endeavor to daily allow Christ to make you over. It is an experience you won't regret!

**GOD BLESS!!!!!!!**